KATE CHOPIN

LITERATURE AND LIFE SERIES
(Formerly Modern Literature and World Dramatists)

Selected list of titles:

SIMONE DE BEAUVOIR *Robert D. Cottrell*
WILLA CATHER *Dorothy Tuck McFarland*
JOAN DIDION *Katherine Usher Henderson*
LILLIAN HELLMAN *Doris V. Falk*
THE NOVELS OF HENRY JAMES *Edward Wagenknecht*
THE TALES OF HENRY JAMES *Edward Wagenknecht*
SARAH ORNE JEWETT *Josephine Donovan*
ANAÏS NIN *Bettina L. Knapp*
JOYCE CAROL OATES *Ellen G. Friedman*
KATHERINE ANNE PORTER *John Edward Hardy*
MARK TWAIN *Robert Keith Miller*
SIMONE WEIL *Dorothy Tuck McFarland*
EUDORA WELTY *Elizabeth Evans*
EDITH WHARTON *Richard H. Lawson*
VIRGINIA WOOLF *Manly Johnson*

Complete list of titles in the series available from publisher on request.

KATE CHOPIN

Barbara C. Ewell

THE UNGAR PUBLISHING COMPANY
NEW YORK

Grateful acknowledgment is made to the Louisiana State University Press for permission to reprint lines from "Because" and "I Wanted God," which appeared originally in *The Complete Works of Kate Chopin*.

Printed in the United States of America

Library of Congress Cataloging-in-Publication Data

Ewell, Barbara C.
Kate Chopin.
(Literature and life series)
Bibliography: p.
Includes index.
1. Chopin, Kate, 1851–1904—Criticism and interpretation. I. Title. II. Series.
PS1294.C63Z64 1986 813′.4 85-28973
ISBN 0-8044-2190-0 (cloth)

For my parents

Ruth Guidry Ewell
and
Dave Haas Ewell, Jr.
—children of bayou folk

Contents

Acknowledgments

It is a pleasure to acknowledge formally the many—sometimes silent—hands who assisted in the shaping of this book. The major part of its research and writing was expedited by a Monticello College Foundation Fellowship for Women, which allowed me six blissfully uninterrupted months at the Newberry Library in Chicago, whose splendid staff (especially Paul Gehl and Richard Brown) and outstanding resources greatly simplified my task. The American Council of Learned Societies also generously funded both my study of Chopin's papers at the Missouri Historical Society in St. Louis and the costs of preparing the manuscript. The University of Mississippi, its Department of English, and its Graduate School provided me with travel monies, faculty research awards, and released time from teaching. I am also indebted to the reading room staff of the Missouri Historical Society, especially Janice Fox and Carol Verble, for their gracious and efficient help. And, of course, no student of Kate Chopin can fail to be indebted to Per Seyersted, whose recovery of Chopin's life and work is the foundation of this study.

No less important despite its unofficial nature—and to which most of the virtues and none of the flaws of this work can be attributed—has been the assistance of friends and colleagues. There were those at the Newberry, for example, whose discussions and interest happily shaped many of my approaches and conclusions; prominent among them were Dominique Marçais, Peter Rudnytsky, Catherine Sklar, John Wands, Catherine Zuckert, and especially Mary Beth Rose and Michael Zuckert, who read and commented on early drafts. I am also grateful to my students, particularly Mary Lynne Warren, in my women in literature classes, who inspired many of my readings. Meanwhile, Joanne Hawks, Carolyn Ellis, Sheila Skemp, and other friends of the Sarah Isom Center for Women's Studies at the University of Mississippi administered essential spiritual and material aid throughout the process. In the final stages, Teresa Toulouse and Benjamin F. Fisher IV provided editorial help, without which this would have been a far less polished product than it is. Emily Toth also read and commented on the final drafts, generously sharing many juicy tidbits of her research. But my best and severest critic, who continually interrupted his own work to help with mine, has been my husband, Jerry Speir. His patience, practical advice, and perennial affection deserve credit for inspiring the best in what follows.

New Orleans, Louisiana
September 1985

Chronology

8 February 1851	Born in St. Louis, Missouri
1 November 1855	Father killed in railroad accident
1855–1868	Attends St. Louis Academy of the Sacred Heart, first as a boarder and then intermittently until graduation
January–February 1863	Deaths of halfbrother, George, and great-grandmother, Victoire Charleville
1867–1870	Keeps commonplace book of quotations and diary entries
1869–1870	Composes first surviving fiction, "Emancipation, A Life Fable"
April 1869	First visit to New Orleans; learns to smoke
9 June 1870	Marries Oscar Chopin in Holy Angels Church, St. Louis
June–September 1870	Keeps journal of wedding trip to Germany, Switzerland, and France
October 1870	Moves to New Orleans, settling on Magazine Street
November 1870	Father-in-law, Victor Jean-Baptiste Chopin, dies

22 May 1871	Son Jean-Baptiste born in New Orleans
1871(?)–1880(?)	Keeps journal seen by Daniel Rankin, now lost
24 September 1873	Son Oscar born in St. Louis
27 December 1873	Brother Tom killed in buggy accident
28 October 1874	Son George born in St. Louis; moves to Constantinople Street residence about this time
26 January 1876	Son Frederick born in New Orleans; moves to 209 [now 1413] Louisiana Avenue
8 January 1878	Son Felix born in New Orleans
31 December 1879	Daughter Lelia born in Cloutierville(?)
1879	Oscar's cotton brokerage fails; family moves to Cloutierville
10 December 1882	Oscar dies from "swamp fever" (malaria)
1882–1884	Runs Cloutierville store and plantations; probable date of brief romantic attachment
1884	Moves family to mother's home at 1122 St. Ange Avenue, St. Louis
June 1885	Mother, Eliza Faris O'Flaherty, dies
1886	Moves to 3317 Morgan Street, St. Louis
June 1887	First visit to Cloutierville after Oscar's death
1888	Reads Maupassant's stories, inspiring her to write "life, not fiction"

1888	Privately publishes "Lilia. Polka for Piano"
1888–1889	Begins first stories, "Euphraisie" and "Grande Isle"
10 January 1889	First publication, a poem, "If It Might Be," in *America*
5 July 1889	Begins first novel, *At Fault*
27 October 1889	First published story, "A Point at Issue!" appears in St. Louis *Post-Dispatch*
19 August 1890	One thousand copies of *At Fault* privately printed by Nixon-Jones
27 November 1890	Completes *Young Dr. Gosse and Theo*
1890–1892	Member of Wednesday Club of St. Louis
1890s	Part of St. Louis literary and publishing circles, including C. L. Deyo, William Marion Reedy, William Schuyler, Henry Dumay, John Dillon, George S. Johns, Sue V. Moore, and Grace Davidson
20 April 1891	Sells "For Marse Chouchoute," soon followed by other Louisiana tales, including "A No-Account Creole," to *Century*
May 1893	Visits Boston to seek a publisher for a "collection of creole stories"
11 August 1893	Houghton Mifflin accepts *Bayou Folk* for publication
14 January 1894	Inaugural issue of *Vogue* features "Désirée's Baby" and "A Visit to Avoyelles"
24 March 1894	*Bayou Folk* published

19 April 1894	Writes "The Story of an Hour," first non-Louisiana story in two years
4 May 1894	Begins "Impressions," diary and notebook
June 1894	Attends Indiana Convention of the Western Association of Writers
July 1894	Vacations at "The Cedars" near Sulphur Springs, Missouri, where she composes "The Night Came Slowly" and "Juanita," rare first-person sketches
October 1894	Preparing second collection of Louisiana stories; writes series of critical essays for St. Louis *Life*
March 1895	Sends collection of Maupassant tales to Houghton Mifflin
November 1896	Submits *A Vocation and a Voice* to Houghton Mifflin
27 January 1897	Grandmother, Athénaïse Charleville Faris, dies
3 February 1897	Meets Ruth McEnery Stuart
February–March 1897	Writes essays for *Criterion*
June 1897–January 1898	Writing *The Awakening*
November 1897	*A Night in Acadie* published by Way and Williams (Chicago)
March 1898	Seeks literary agent
18 July 1898	Writes "The Storm," without attempting to publish it
November 1898	*A Night in Acadie*, *A Vocation and a Voice*, and *The Awakening* transferred from Way and Williams to H. S. Stone, successor of Stone and Kimball

January 1899	"In the Confidence of a Story-Writer" appears in *Atlantic Monthly*
22 April 1899	*The Awakening* published by Herbert S. Stone
4 May 1899	First review by Frances Porcher
28 May 1899	Retraction written for July issue of *Book News*
October 1899	Travels to Wisconsin lake country; receives forged letter from "Janet Scammon Young"
26 November 1899	Laudatory essay appears in St. Louis *Post-Dispatch*
29 November 1899	Reading of "Ti Démon" to Wednesday Club
December–January 1900	Last visit to Louisiana
16 January 1900	W. B. Parker of *Atlantic* rejects "Ti Démon"
February 1900	*A Vocation and a Voice* returned by H. S. Stone
April 1900	"The White Eagle" and "An Egyptian Cigarette" accepted by *Vogue*
October 1901	Writes three stories; sells only "The Woodchoppers"
14 January 1902	Writes "Polly," last story published in her lifetime
1903	Moves to 4232 McPherson Avenue; health failing
20 August 1904	Attends "Pennsylvania Day" at the St. Louis World Exposition; is stricken by cerebral hemorrhage later in the evening
22 August 1904	Dies around noon

24 August 1904	Buried from St. Louis's New Cathedral Chapel; interred in Calvary Cemetery
1906	*The Awakening* and *Bayou Folk* reissued
1911	*Bayou Folk* reissued
1932	Daniel S. Rankin's biography published: *Kate Chopin and Her Creole Stories*
1964	*The Awakening* reissued by Capricorn; introduction by Kenneth Eble
1969	Per Seyersted publishes *The Complete Works of Kate Chopin* and *Kate Chopin: A Critical Biography*
1979	Publication of *A Kate Chopin Miscellany*, eds. Per Seyersted and Emily Toth

Introduction

Since its publication in 1899, *The Awakening* has been the touchstone of Kate Chopin's literary reputation. Chopin's national prominence as a local colorist, with two successful short-story collections to her credit, was instantly overshadowed by this unassuming tale of an undistinguished woman trapped by a conventional nineteenth-century marriage. Greeted by a storm of protest over its "unseemly" treatment of adultery, the novel drew its author into disrepute—and disappointment. Within a year of its hostile reception, a disheartened Kate Chopin was writing fewer and fewer stories, and by her death in 1904, she had all but ceased to write.

Although *The Awakening* was Chopin's last major work, neither its fate nor hers was quite sealed by its inauspicious beginnings. Like most other tempests, the uproar eventually faded. *The Awakening* went out of print and was only briefly reissued in 1906, after Chopin's death. In the period of relative silence that followed, Chopin received only limited notice as a local colorist in critical surveys of American literature; frequently, her notorious novel was not even mentioned.[1] Even F. L. Pattee, who in 1923 described her stories as the work of genius, feared that the current eclipse of her talent was "destined to be total."[2] That darkness was somewhat diminished by Daniel Rankin's important 1932 biography *Kate Chopin and Her Creole Stories*, based on inter with her acquaintances and surviving family members. But Rankin's effort to reestablish Chopin's reputation still slighted *The Awakening* as an unfortunate anomaly of her canon.[3] It was French critic Cyrille Arnavon, writing on American realism in 1946, who finally acknowledged the significant achievement of Chopin's last novel. Though Arnavon found fault with motivation and with the novel's "artificial and obviously deliberate" structure, he praised its vivid characters and psychological realism.[4] Arnavon's critical rehabilitation was followed by a scattering of appreciative commentators in the 1950s and 1960s, and in 1964 Kenneth Eble's edition of *The Awakening* appeared—the first in fifty-eight years.[5] Five years later, Per Seyersted published the important *Complete Works* and his *Kate Chopin: A Critical Biography.*[6] The long obscurity of Kate Chopin's work was coming to an end.

It was not wholly fortuitous and certainly not inconsequential that the recovery of *The Awakening* and Kate Chopin coincided with the latest rebirth of the women's movement. When the novel was written (the same year Charlotte Perkins Gilman's *Women and Economics* appeared), American women were grappling with many of the problems that have been rearticulated in the last two decades: what is woman's role? how does patriarchy limit female selfhood and sexuality? to what extent does gender restrict personal freedom? Reprinted in *Redbook* in 1972 as a "classic underground novel," *The Awakening* expressed the persistence and continuing power of these issues for a new era.

A slim volume, its original light green binding finely adorned with graceful, wine-dark vines, *The Awakening* has always possessed a disproportionate power in Chopin's canon. Much of the critical work that has followed its revival, for example, has either isolated it or attempted to read back into Chopin's earlier fiction the themes that it so vividly expressed. But while we must understand this masterpiece in the context of Chopin's brief career as a writer of short fiction, we should also try to avoid reading backward. Chopin's short fiction certainly does anticipate the achievement and themes of her last novel, but its own intrinsic merits and concerns can be better appreciated if the light of *The Awakening* is not too blinding. The short fiction, in fact, casts shadows that can better define the novel's own fine contours. Toward such a result this present study strives: to view the work of Kate Chopin in its entirety, so that her famous novel appears as an inescapable climax, but not the sum of her achievement as a writer.

Some mention should be made of the organization that follows. Although a strictly chronological study of her stories as they were written might illumine certain patterns of Chopin's thought, it would also obscure the relative integrity of her three collections—especially the first—and the influence of successful publication on her career. As her experience with *The Awakening* dramatizes, Chopin was sensitive to public opinion; just as she later retired under reproach, she had earlier blossomed with encouragement and success. This response was particularly true with the publication of *Bayou Folk*, her first and most successful short-story collection, which gathered what Chopin thought was her best and most saleable local-color fiction from the previous three years. Since her identity as a writer was firmly linked to this book and since its success apparently generated a very powerful current in her subsequent fiction, it is treated as a whole. For despite its wide-ranging chronology, the impact of *Bayou Folk* on Chopin's fiction is greater as a successful book than as a series of tales. The uncollected stories of the same period are then discussed in this context.

While such a format loosely governs each chapter, the discussions gradually become more chronological, because after *A Night in Acadie* (which included a final gleaning of earlier Louisiana stories), the directions taken in Chopin's work become more readily discernible when her tales are examined in the sequence of their composition. Such an arrangement reveals an obvious compromise between strict chronology and the impact of public responses to Chopin's stories. As such, it represents an effort to clarify the extent to which Chopin's development as a writer was affected not only by private literary decisions but also by her reactions to public appraisals of her work. One further note: the composition dates of Chopin's stories, which she usually entered in her logbooks, are indicated in parentheses when the story is first discussed. Quotations from Seyersted's *Complete Works* are abbreviated as CW. However, since there are so many current editions of *The Awakening*, I have preferred chapter references for quotations of that novel.

1

St. Louis Woman, Louisiana Writer

The Louisiana Purchase Exposition of 1904 was a grand event in the life of St. Louis: there were exhibits from sixty-two countries; exotic people in native dress; art work by Rembrandt, Rousseau, Turner, and Rodin; and all the most important inventions of the new century—electricity, automobiles, flying machines.

As an enthusiastic supporter of the fair, Kate Chopin had purchased one of the first season's tickets. Virtually a daily visitor, she was there on Saturday, August 20, Pennsylvania Day. A violent rainstorm had drenched the city the night before, but by mid-morning, a dog days' sun was creating one of the fair's steamiest days. In declining health for about a year, Chopin returned from the day's exertions tired, but content. The fair, she insisted, always lifted her spirits. By midnight that evening, however, a severe headache caused her to summon her son Jean. By the time he reached her bedside, she was unconscious, her brain hemorrhaging. As her children gathered, she rallied briefly Sunday afternoon and recognized another son, George, but again fell unconscious. She died around noon on the next day, August 22, and was buried two days later in Calvary Cemetery.[1]

By all accounts, Kate Chopin was a remarkable, charming person. Not very tall, inclined to be plump, and quite pretty, she had thick, wavy brown hair that grayed prematurely, and direct, sparkling brown eyes. Her friends remembered most her quiet manner and quick Irish wit, embellished with a gift for mimicry. A gracious, easygoing hostess, she enjoyed laughter, music, and dancing, but especially intellectual talk, and she could express her own considered opinions with surprising directness.

Chopin's ethnic heritage was French and Irish. Her mother, Eliza Faris, was an intelligent and vigorous woman descended from two of St. Louis's oldest Creole families. Eliza's maternal grandmother was Victoire Verdon Charleville, born in 1780, whose own mother, Marianne Victoire Richelet Verdon, had operated a line of keelboats between St. Louis and New Orleans.[2]

Eliza was just sixteen when she wed Thomas O'Flaherty, an up-and-coming Irish immigrant more than twice her age. Born in County Galway in 1805, O'Flaherty emigrated to America in 1823; two years later he settled in the bustling little town of St. Louis and eventually established himself as a merchant for the expanding river traffic. In 1839, he married the daughter of a well-known Creole family, Catherine deReilhe, who died a few years after the birth of their son George. In 1844 Thomas was married a second time, to the young Eliza Faris.

Into the O'Flahertys' spacious home on then fashionable Eighth Street were born their children: in 1848, Thomas, Jr., who was killed at twenty-five in a buggy accident; Katherine, on February 8, 1851; Jane, and finally Marie Thérèse, who both died quite young. Evidently the household also included Eliza's mother, Athénaïse Charleville Faris, with her five youngest children, and later Kate's great-grandmother, Victoire Charleville.[3] Then, in November 1855, Thomas O'Flaherty was killed when the special train of dignitaries and stockholders inaugurating the Pacific Railroad was wrecked on the Gasconade River bridge. The disaster transformed the bustling O'Flaherty residence into a house of pious widows and children.

Kate's mother's widowhood at twenty-seven evidently drew her closer to her daughter, forging an intimacy that lasted until Eliza's death. But Kate's great-grandmother also significantly influenced her young favorite's education and upbringing. By insisting that the child speak French and learn the piano, Madame Charleville fostered two lifelong devotions. A third was encouraged by Madame's vivid tales of early St. Louis settlers, the seamier details of which her great-granddaughter was instructed not to judge—"God did that."[4]

The years of the Civil War were troubling for the O'Flahertys. They were Southern sympathizers, and young George eventually slipped past the Union occupation to join the Confederate Army. Kate herself became St. Louis's "Littlest Rebel" when, as she later recalled, she "tore down the union flag from the front porch when the Yanks tied it up there" (CW, 716). She outwitted the ensuing Union search by hiding the offending material in a bag of scraps, and a childhood friend remembered that her arrest was avoided only "by the kind, timely interference of a neighborly . . . physician [who was] a strong Unionist."[5] But more solemn events soon followed: George was captured and exchanged, only to die of typhoid fever in Arkansas on his way back to his regiment, his untimely death following closely that of Mme. Charleville on January 16, 1863.

These difficult losses for twelve-year-old Kate were surely intensified by the wartime absence of her close friend, Kitty Garesché. The girls had met at the St. Louis Academy of the Sacred Heart, where Kate's formal education had begun in 1855 as a boarder and continued intermittently. Conducted by the Society of the Sacred Heart, the academy instructed the daughters of the city's best Catholic families in a vigorous European curriculum of religion, languages, literature, and the sciences, as well as domestic and social skills. Of their schooldays, Kitty Garesché later recalled that she and Kate were avid readers, sharing "mid laughter and tears" popular romances like *Blind Agnes*, *Paul and Virginia*, *Queechy*, *Wide Wide World*, *Zaidee*, and *John Halifax, Gentleman*, as well as Dickens, Scott, Grimm, and *Pilgrim's Progress*. Such eclectic reading habits only expanded as Kate matured.

Kate's own record of her literary tastes is preserved in a commonplace book she kept from 1867 to 1870. Containing both lists and excerpts of books, it includes several early compositions. For the most part, the writings are predictably adolescent: a flowery lament on the death of a young contemporary, a pious comparison of Christian and pagan art, a sentimental poem on the joys of the past and the fear of an unknown future, a witty poem about feast-day celebrations at school. There are also glimpses of her vibrant and opinionated character. The exercise on "The Congé," for example, contains a humorous self-characterization:

> While Katie O'F, poor unfortunate lass,
> Broke implements stoutest as though they were glass.

Other comments confirm her affection for music and her belief in its power to awaken "the slumbering passions in the heart of man." And even at seventeen, she was describing with telling care the character of the "famous violinist Ole Bull" whose concert she had attended:

> His age I should judge to be between sixty and seventy; but though old he is still handsome—tall straight and robust. His countenance is excessively pleasing; his hair of an iron gray; and his whole appearance that of a gentleman of the old school. He handles his instrument, as I thought, tenderly, as though it were something he loved, and in his performance is perfectly

at ease—displaying nothing of that exaggerated style most usually seen in fine violinists.[6]

Elsewhere, we observe her opinionated dislike of Fontenelle, her orthodox disappointment at Macaulay's failure to appreciate Catholicism, her admiration for Longfellow, her fascination for all things German, and her frustrations with serial stories. Her complaints about the brand-new *Appleton's Journal*, whose story by Victor Hugo had absorbed her, indicate that her reading was as current as it was wide.

Kate's reflective nature is also evident in her journal. There were the "blue days" of adolescence when her usual occupations ("Reading, music, German, walking, skating") held little appeal. She also found herself at odds that winter of 1868 with the hectic whirl of her first social season. Having graduated from the academy in June, Kate had become, according to her friend William Schuyler, "one of the acknowledged belles of St. Louis, a favorite not only for her beauty, but also for her amiability of character and her cleverness."[7] But her ambivalence about that life-style is evident in one of her most intimate entries, written near the end of that first season, on Holy Thursday, 1869. Feeling idle and a bit cross, she contemplates the end of Lent with its renewal of "parties—theatres, and general spreeing," the endless dancing with men she despises, and the exhaustion of her body and brain:

> I am a creature who loves amusements; I love brightness and gaiety and life and sunshine. But is it a rational amusement, I ask myself, to destroy one's health, and turn night into day?

Her uneasiness about these contradictions expands to a more general uncertainty:

> Heigh ho! I wish this were the *only* subject I have doubts upon. One does become so tired—reasoning, reasoning, reasoning,

from morning till night and coming to no conclusions—it is to say the least slightly unsatisfactory.

She goes on to berate her hypocrisy toward bores and her chagrin at learning "the art of making oneself agreeable in conversation . . . to look pleased and chagrined, surprised, indignant and under *every* circumstance—interested and entertained." Clearly, Kate's perceptions of human nature were becoming well developed.

Her ability to sketch people and places with brevity and humor recurs in the next entry, which describes her traveling companions on her first visit to New Orleans later that year:

> Not remarkably gay for me when one reflects that Mother is a few years older than myself—Rosie an invalid—Mrs. Sloan a walking breathing nonentity—Mamie a jovial giggler and Nina a child.—N. Orleans I liked immensely; it is so clean—so white and green. Although in April, we had profusions of flowers—strawberries and even black berries.[8]

The entry continues with a description of the highlight of the trip—a visit with a talented German socialite and singer whose public success the lively eighteen-year-old obviously admired. After the return to St. Louis, however, the journal is almost exclusively extracts, though the writers are as various as Lamartine and Seneca, Dinah Maria (Craik) Mulock and Washington Irving.

About this time, Kate also completed a brief sketch, perhaps her first real fiction, entitled "Emancipation, A Life Fable," which she carefully preserved. The fable describes the fate of a once contented animal who, when accidentally released, prefers the dangers of freedom to its caged security. The animal experiences a sensuous thrill at real life, "seeing, smelling, touching of all things . . . seeking, finding, joying and suffering." With its rich, sensuous evocations and its insistence on emancipation from even comfortable constraint once "the spell of the Unknown" (CW, 37–38) is asserted, the piece is a provocative inaugural of its author's later career. Doubtless it expresses her excitement at her own irrevocable entry into adulthood, and, perhaps, love. The latter is hinted in a journal entry recorded nearly a year after the New Orleans visit: "In two weeks," she muses, "I am going to be married; married to the right man. . . . And how surprised every one was, for I had kept it so secret!"[9]

The "right man" was twenty-five-year-old Oscar Chopin, the son of a French-Creole family from Natchitoches [Nak-i-tush] Parish in northwestern Louisiana. The couple had met at Oakland, the country estate near St. Louis of Louis A. Benoist, Oscar's distant relative whose banking methods he had come north to learn. Oscar's father, Victor Jean-Baptiste Chopin, was a physician who had emigrated from France in the 1840s. He promptly married the daughter of a good French family, Julia Benoist of Cloutierville. J. B. Chopin was a hard and acquisitive man. Though constantly enlarging his land and business holdings, he virtually isolated his wife and once tried to force his more gentle-tempered son to oversee his harshly treated slaves. When the Civil War broke out, he fled with his family to France, where in their six years abroad, Oscar completed his education. When the family returned to Louisiana after the war, they resettled in New Orleans for the sake of Julia's health. But Oscar's mother died in April 1870, shortly after her son had become engaged to Kate O'Flaherty.

The couple was married in Holy Angels Church on June 9, 1870—the "happiest day of my life," as the bride exclaims in the honeymoon diary that continues her journal.[10] The new Mrs. Chopin's record of their three-month holiday abroad is her most extensive personal account to survive; unfortunately, it discloses more about her itinerary than about herself. Nonetheless, there are noteworthy incidents and details of her impressions. We

find her, for example, an enthusiastic, and often amusingly critical, traveler. Philadelphia she pronounces "a gloomy puritanical looking city"; New York "a great den of swindlers" and "dull, dull"; Cologne generally unattractive; but she thinks Bremen, Heidelberg, and Switzerland charming, and she positively effuses about the Rhine. There are also hints of independence, of her self-confidence about being a married woman with a new freedom to explore, and a sample of her attitudes toward feminism. When one of the Clafflin sisters, "the notorious 'female broker'" and noted feminist, exhorts her on the train to "elevate my mind" with "politics, commerce, questions of state, etc, etc.," Chopin good-naturedly assures her that she will. Later she reports that the New York Stock Exchange "interested me very much." In Bonn, she is miffed that even her married status won't get her into the halls where the male students congregated. Later, after rowing a boat on Lake Geneva, she proudly recounts "handling the oars quite like an expert"; and that afternoon, as Oscar is napping, she takes a walk alone:

> How very far I *did* go . . . I wonder what people thought of me—a young woman strolling about alone. I even took a glass of beer at a friendly little beer garden quite on the edge of the lake.[11]

The modest daring of such little adventures previews the venturesomeness evident in her later life and work. The Chopins' honeymoon, however, was cut short by the outbreak of the Franco-Prussian war. And after witnessing the fall of the Second Empire in Paris, they hurried back to New York and St. Louis where, as the last line of the diary records, "once again I have embraced those dear ones left behind."

Chopin's stay in her native city was brief. In October she moved with her husband to New Orleans where they settled on Magazine Street on the American side of the city. This fact, plus her Irish ancestry, did not please her peevish, Francophile father-in-law, but her self-assurance and command of French quickly won him over. When he died in November 1870, he appeared quite reconciled to his new daughter-in-law, already pregnant with her first child. His namesake, Jean-Baptiste, was born in May 1871—an event Chopin recalled twenty-three years later in a second surviving diary:

> I can remember yet that hot southern day on Magazine street in New Orleans. The noises of the street coming through the open windows; that heaviness with which I dragged myself about; my husband's and mother's solicitude; old Alexandrine the quadroon nurse with her high bandana tignon, her hoop-earrings and placid smile; old Doctor Faget; the smell of chloroform, and then waking at 6 in the evening from out of a stupor to see in my mothers arms a little piece of humanity all dressed in white which they told me was my little son! The sensation with which I touched my lips and my finger tips to his soft flesh only comes once to a mother. It must be the pure animal sensation; nothing spiritual could be so real—so poignant.[12]

This vivid and startlingly sensuous account of childbirth reveals the acute sensory awareness that Chopin was constantly incorporating into her fiction—often with equally startling effects. Jean-Baptiste was followed by five more children: Oscar on September 24, 1873; George, October 28, 1874—all born in St. Louis—then Frederick, January 26, 1876; Felix, January 8, 1878, and her only daughter, Lelia, December 31, 1879.[13]

The Chopins' life in New Orleans was pleasant. Oscar's business as a cotton factor prospered, and they moved several times to more commodious lodgings, finally to 209 Louisiana Avenue, now the state headquarters of a women's historical association. The family also made frequent, sometimes prolonged visits to St. Louis, and often spent summers (when yellow fever most threatened) at Grande Isle, then a fashionable Creole coastal resort about ninety miles from New Orleans and later a principal setting of *The Awakening*.

By every account, Oscar and Kate were a fond and loving couple. Oscar was an indulgent husband and parent, rather stout and of a naturally jovial disposition, enjoying conversation and company, and perhaps not a little wary of his father's harsh treatment of his mother. Despite his family's indignant criticism of his supposed inability to make his wife conform to the stuffy standards of Creole society, Oscar never restrained her behavior. Indeed, he seemed to enjoy it, especially her droll mimicry of those very relatives and whatever else captured her fancy.

Kate's independent attitude must have been a trial to her husband's more traditional circle. According to a diary of the period, which is now lost, she was especially fond of roaming about the city alone, an unconventional activity for women. She often walked or rode the mule-drawn streetcars, observing the cosmopolitan bustle of the French Market or Canal Street or the waterfront, where her husband's—and earlier her father's—business originated. Though her notes on these sights were evidently not deliberately literary, they indicated the sources of the fiction that was to come.[14] Another unusual habit Kate continued was smoking cigarettes. Though she had learned to smoke on her first visit to New Orleans in 1869, she tried not to offend openly those who disapproved. She also enjoyed distinctive apparel and was remembered by her Cloutierville neighbors a few years later as wearing "tight fitting clothes, . . . chic hats and a good deal of lavender colors in all her costumes." An account of her favorite riding costume from that period recalls

> a fantastic affair—a close-fitting riding habit of blue cloth, the train fastened up at the side to disclose an embroidered skirt,

and the little feet encased in pretty boots with high heels. A jaunty little jockey hat and feather, and buff gloves rendered her charming.[15]

The cotton yields of 1878–1879 were very poor. Oscar Chopin's brokerage failed, and that winter he moved his young brood to his family's estate at Cloutierville. The peculiar geography of the area was to be richly incorporated into his wife's later fiction. The little village of the Benoists was on the Cane River about twenty miles south of Natchitoches, itself the oldest town in the Louisiana Purchase. The former bed of the Red River, the Cane had been deserted above Natchitoches at Grand Écore in the floods of 1832 for a stream a few miles east, the Rigolets de Bon Dieu. The Cane still carried considerable traffic, especially in high water, though it was no longer the region's principal waterway. Cloutierville was a single strip of twenty or thirty frame houses beside the river, anchored at one end by the Catholic Church, St. John's, and on the other by the former home of Oscar's grandmother, where the Chopins took up residence. Restored by Mildred McCoy in the early 1970s as the Bayou Folk Museum, the house was built by Alexis Cloutier in the early 1800s: a gracious two-story "Louisiana-type" structure, made of cypress and brick, with broad porches and generous windows. Nearby was the Chopin plantation, whose previous owner, Robert McAlpin, many identified with Simon Legree, a tradition to which Kate Chopin later alluded in *At Fault*.[16]

In addition to running some small, local plantations, Oscar bought a general store in Cloutierville, which his generous credit quickly made popular. Since the Chopin family was well established in the area, Oscar and Kate were readily absorbed into a relaxed and abundant social life. Though Kate was sometimes as startling to Cloutierville as she had been to the Vieux Carré with her love of horseback riding—which the townspeople never understood—and her eccentric riding clothes, she evidently fitted well into the life of the village. Certainly, the people of the Cane River country made a powerful and sympathetic impression on her. As her daughter later wrote, Chopin's daily relations with these "simple people" taught her to love as well as know them, "for no matter how keenly they appealed to her wonderful sense of humor, she always touched on their weaknesses fondly and tolerantly, never unkindly."[17]

However, this comfortable life ended abruptly. On December 10, 1882, Oscar died of swamp fever.[18] Kate Chopin was thirty-two, with six children under twelve, her youngest not yet three. Her independent spirit now manifested its practical dimensions. Her friend William Schuyler later wrote that "having rejected all offers of assistance from kindly relatives," Chopin energetically

> undertook the management of her plantations and developed much ability as a business woman. She had to carry on correspondence with the cotton factors in New Orleans, make written contracts, necessitating many personal interviews with the poorer creoles, the Acadians, and the "free mulattoes," who raised the crop "on shares," see that the plantation store was well stocked, and sometimes even, in emergencies, keep shop herself. It was hard work. . . .[19]

Chopin remained in Louisiana for more than a year, managing her affairs with notable success, including, very likely, a romantic attachment to a prominent Cloutierville man.[20] But her mother's constant urgings finally prevailed, and the family moved into the St. Ange Street house in St. Louis in 1884. Hardly a year passed, however, before Chopin's mother also died.

Kate Chopin was, her biographers concur, "prostrate with grief." No immediate relatives survived to share her losses except her seventy-four-year-old grandmother, Athénaïse Charleville, and six demanding young children. Chopin's daughter recalled the melancholy that thereafter tempered her mother's natural good spirits:

When I speak of my mother's keen sense of humor and of her habit of looking on the amusing side of everything, I don't want to give you the impression of her being joyous, for she was on the contrary rather a sad nature. She was undemonstrative both in grief and happiness, but her feelings were very deep as is usual with such natures. I think the tragic death of her father early in her life, of her much loved brothers, the loss of her young husband and her mother, left a stamp of sadness on her which was never lost.[21]

Economically at least, Chopin was reasonably secure. Though much of her mother's estate had been swindled by an unscrupulous friend, she retained a modest income from several St. Louis properties as well as Oscar's Natchitoches Parish holdings.[22] In 1886 she moved from her mother's residence to 3317 Morgan Street in the newer, western part of St. Louis. It was to be her home for the next seventeen years and the birthplace of her writing career.

One person who proved especially supportive in these difficult years was Dr. Frederick Kolbenheyer. A frequent visitor at her new address, Kolbenheyer had delivered several of Chopin's children—one of whom was his namesake—and was, in Rankin's words, "a cordially accepted intimate friend, almost an ardent admirer of Kate Chopin."[23] His influence on her was decided, both personally and professionally. Having emigrated from Austria in 1870, Kolbenheyer was a forceful personality with radical opinions, and he encouraged her acquaintance with philosophers like Kant, Hegel, and Schopenhauer, his own specialties. Even while running the plantations, Chopin had never ceased her reading habits, and her learned friend must have provided a lively sounding board for her thoughts on science and the works of Darwin, Huxley, and Spencer, of which she was especially fond.[24] Kolbenheyer's determined agnosticism may also have influenced Chopin's withdrawal from Catholicism, which she virtually ceased to practice within a year after her mother's death. But surely the doctor's most important effect on her life was his encouragement of her literary talents. He had received several of her letters from Louisiana, and, impressed with their literary quality, he now urged her to try writing fiction. Whether for distraction or income, Chopin took his advice, and, sometime in 1888, she began her first story, "Euphraisie."

Though her first publication, in January 1889, was a faintly autobiographical poem, "If It Might Be," and though she began a novel the same year, Chopin soon found her métier in the short story.

Primarily an American form, with influential infusions from the French, the genre was rapidly adding respectability to the broad currency it had achieved in the 1870s and 1880s, encouraged by the steady growth of magazines in the second half of the century. To a society eager for self-improvement and for more national, if not exactly cosmopolitan, perspectives, the magazines were highly accommodating. Filled with essays on science and philosophy, morality and politics, even general-interest journals also included a great deal of literature – not only serialized novels (which had been popular since the eighteenth century) but also short fiction, much of it written in the new mode of local color. Several prominent editors, including William Dean Howells at *Atlantic Monthly* and R. W. Gilder at *Century*, had encouraged this fashion particularly because it often embodied the realistic principles they supported.

That Chopin should turn her talents to local-color tales was as much a practical as an artistic decision. On the one hand, the lively demand for such stories would lead to publication and recognition more quickly than the less readily publishable novel, whose difficulties she had experienced in her first attempt at that genre. More important, however, the short story had provided Chopin with the major inspiration of her writing career, Guy de Maupassant. This young Frenchman, a disciple of

Flaubert, had taken the literary world by storm in 1880 with his short fiction. Marked by an impeccable, concise prose, carefully chosen, expressive details, and solidly realistic characters, often drawn from the lower classes, his tales opened new vistas in the art of the *conte* or *novelle.* For Chopin, who claimed to have "stumbled upon Maupassant" around 1888, they were a revelation:

> I read his stories and marvelled at them. Here was life, not fiction; for where were the plots, the old fashioned mechanism and stage trapping that in a vague, unthinking way I had fancied were essential to the art of story making. Here was a man who had escaped from tradition and authority, who had entered into himself and looked out upon life through his own being and with his own eyes; and who, in a direct and simple way, told us what he saw. When a man does this, he gives us the best that he can; something valuable for it is genuine and spontaneous. He gives us his impressions (CW, 700–701).

What Chopin learned from Maupassant is evident in her stories: her own clear prose; her pointed use of details; the solid, authentic folk that populate her fiction. She also adapted—and used effectively—the surprise ending, for which Maupassant is most often remembered. But what seems to have most impressed Chopin was not so much his technique as his clear-spirited commitment to a unique vision of life: "what he saw." Groping about in the painful years after her husband's and mother's deaths, "making my own acquaintance," she doubtless found in his work a needed confirmation of her own perspectives as well as a validation of their expression. Certainly the two short-story writers whom she later singled out for praise, Sarah Orne Jewett and Mary E. Wilkins Freeman, possessed a similar confidence in their experience, writing of New England life with a perception and honesty that gave their fiction the effect of real life—as they saw it.

Chopin's initial choice of subject, then, the people

of south Louisiana, was at once an imaginary indulgence in her happiest memories and an expression of her literary faith in the legitimacy of a personal vision. That faith is evident both in her approach to composition and in her impressionistic style. Though some of the revised manuscripts that survive belie her announced perfunctoriness in matters of craftsmanship, Chopin was clearly confident in the immediate power of the imagination. "Story-writing," as she once described it,

> is the spontaneous expression of impressions gathered goodness knows where. . . . I am completely at the mercy of unconscious selection. To such an extent is this true, that what is called the polishing up process has always proved disastrous to my work, and I avoid it, preferring the integrity of crudities to artificialities (CW, 722).

Her son Felix confirms this process, observing that "the short story burst from her. . . . [She would] go weeks and weeks without an idea, then suddenly grab her pencil and old lapboard . . . and in a couple of hours her story was complete and off to the publisher."[25]

Though such an approach might appear naive or careless — a view Chopin seems sometimes to encourage — there are other possibilities. Although many of her stories — but certainly not all — were in their final form, or very near it, when first drafted, considerable evidence indicates that her seemingly spontaneous compositions were often preceded by long periods of reflection and incubation; that, in fact, her sketches grew out of a rather complex vision of interrelated themes, interconnected incidents, and recurring characters. For example, Hector Santien in "In and Out of Old Natchitoches," written in February 1893, remarks on the coming marriage of "little Athénaïse Miché" — whose own story Chopin doesn't tell until April 1895. The whole Santien saga, completed late in 1893 (with "In Sabine"), must have been considered by Chopin even as she was creating the brothers in *At Fault* in 1890, or even earlier in the 1888 version of "A No-Account Creole." Chopin's many recurring characters – Gouvernail, who first emerges in the January 1894 story "A Respectable Woman," to reappear both in "Athénaïse" (1895) and *The Awakening* (1897); the Laballières of "At the 'Cadian Ball" (1892), "In and Out of Old Natchitoches" (1893), and "The Storm" (1898); or Bud Aiken of "In Sabine" and "Ti Frère" (1896) – indicate the continuities in her fiction. Her apparent deprecation of her art is also partly a response to the contradictory role assigned to women writers of the nineteenth century, especially those of Southern traditions. Reluctantly accepted as professionals, they were enjoined not to allow their essential femininity to be overwhelmed by their supposedly "masculine" literary activity. The difficulty of such a position for serious writers might well elicit a remark like Chopin's flippant equation of housework and writing in an important public statement she made in 1899:

> I write in the morning, when not too strongly drawn to struggle with the intricacies of a pattern, and in the afternoon, if the temptation to try a new furniture polish on an old table leg is not too powerful to be denied; sometimes at night, though as I grow older I am more and more inclined to believe that night was made for sleep (CW, 721–722).

In October 1899, Kate Chopin had already violated several taboos about women's writings, and she was doubtless eager to restore her credibility both as a woman and as an artist. Nevertheless, the wry, ironic tone of the essay does not conceal her resentment at an audience that would reject her most serious art. As she adds near the end: "Sometimes I feel as if I should like to get a good, remunerative job to do the thinking for some people." Writing, arguably, *is* doing "the thinking for some people," even if not always "a good, remunerative job." And as a writer of considerable intellect and power,

Chopin approached her work quite seriously, even when she had to mask that intent with indifference.

Chopin's ideal of aesthetic spontaneity also suggests why she found the local colorist's sketch or short tale so congenial; its directness and brevity were exactly suited to her inspired glimpses of experience and their rapid transcription into fiction. Her compositional habits, moreover, reinforced the impressionistic informality of her style. Spare and direct, with a preponderance of simple declarative statements, it conveys, at its best, precisely the clarity of vision she admired in Maupassant or in the more effusive Whitman. Occasionally seeming naive or artless, her prose is incisive in its use of telling detail and careful understatement. Such bareness and force remarkably anticipate Anderson and Hemingway in the next century.

Of course, Chopin's first stories only promised her eventual achievement, but the essentials were in place. Encouraged by Kolbenheyer and other friends in St. Louis's circle of talented journalists, Chopin began to write—and publish—regularly. In keeping with her sense of artistic integrity, however, she resisted others' overt influences on her fiction. In a short piece written for *Atlantic Monthly* in 1896, she expressed her distrust of "gratuitous advice bandied about, regardless of personal aptitude and wholly confusing to the individual point of view." Recalling her abject failure when she tried to "take pains" in following the current fads of historical romance, she concludes that each writer must "be content to use his own faculty, whether it be a faculty for taking pains or a faculty for reaching his effects by the most careless methods" (CW, 704–5). For Chopin, the fidelity to her own way was as essential to her craft as to her philosophy of life.

Even so, Chopin obviously appreciated the friendship and respect of people like writer and critic William Marion Reedy; editors Sue V. Moore, Alexander De

Menil and Grace Davidson; Henry Dumay, a progressive French professor at Washington University and later editor of the *Criterion*; and the aggressive newspaper editors and journalists: John Dillon, C. L. Deyo, George Johns, and Florence Hayward. In fact, Chopin's home was a frequent gathering place for such interesting folk, and she became, one of them wrote, "closer to maintaining a salon than any woman that has ever lived in St. Louis."[26] Her visiting day, Thursday, often found her unpretentious parlor crowded with interesting and admiring friends. She was even briefly a member of the Wednesday Club, a serious-minded women's organization founded by several prominent intellectuals, including Charlotte Eliot, a noted biographer and the mother of T. S. Eliot. While Chopin was at the center of this vigorous intellectual life of St. Louis in the 1880s, however, the city itself remained essentially Western, with few ties to the more sophisticated cultural centers of the East. And compared with contemporary figures like Howells, Jewett, Twain, or James, whose literary exchanges were intense, Chopin was relatively isolated from the prominent writers of her time, a factor of importance to her later career.

In addition to writing and her social interests, Chopin found time for a good deal of other entertainment. She called herself "something of a euchre fiend" and delighted in organizing musicales, attending concerts and plays, vacationing along the Meramec River south of St. Louis, enjoying the company of her children and their friends, and, of course, reading. An attractive and still quite marriageable widow, Chopin was also the object of some serious courtship, though she apparently encouraged none of her suitors. Whether out of devotion to Oscar or pleasure in the relative independence of widowhood, she evidently found her children and her writing satisfying enough.

By 1893 Chopin was publishing regularly in national magazines like *Youth's Companion*, *Harper's Young*

People, and the new *Vogue*. In January 1894 she made her debut in the prestigious *Century* with a revised version of her very first story, retitled "A No-Account Creole." That same spring, Houghton Mifflin published her first collection of short stories, *Bayou Folk*, and its national success encouraged her most creative period. For the next four years she wrote and published some of her finest short fiction, culminating in a second collection, *A Night in Acadie*, late in 1897. That year, however, was one of significant change. In January, her grandmother—nearly ninety and the closest relative whom her writing might offend—had died. With a third collection of non-Louisiana stories, *A Vocation and a Voice*, then making the rounds, Chopin began a new novel in June. Though short stories had been her medium for several years, she had noted earlier that she did "not consider one form of more value than the other." Evidently persuaded by Horace Scudder's recent encouragement "to write a downright novel,"[27] she thus began her most daring project to date, *The Awakening*.

Kate Chopin was then forty-six and at the peak of her creative powers. Her fiction was widely known; she was the leading figure in St. Louis's "working literary colony," as the *Star-Times* noted in 1898;[28] she had a comfortable circle of interesting, influential friends; and she had successfully reared six children to adulthood, or nearly so. She obviously felt ready to flex her fictive powers and to take a further step toward the full expression of "what [s]he saw"—as Maupassant had first challenged her to do nearly ten years before.

The Awakening was finished in January 1898 but not published until April 22, 1899. In the interim, Chopin wrote a few very experimental stories and a number of poems. Less than two weeks after the new novel appeared, Frances Porcher, an acquaintance of Chopin and assistant editor at the St. Louis *Mirror*, wrote the first review. Though she praised Chopin's artistry,

Porcher condemned her heroine's lack of integrity and wondered aloud if such fiction were worthwhile: "It leaves one sick of human nature and so one would wonder, *cui bono?*" The effect on Chopin was chilling, intensified by the quick succession of similar reviews that soon appeared across the country. Her new novel was a scandal. Alexander De Menil, the most conservative of her editor friends, refused even to review it in his *Hyperion*.

Chopin's dismay was understandable. The enthusiastic letters from her friends—which she carefully preserved—and even a generous commendation from England (possibly forged by her admirers) could not ease her disappointment. Even more cutting perhaps was the personal disapprobation she began to experience. Social acquaintances and even some friends began to avoid her; the city's Mercantile Library reportedly banned the novel from its shelves; she was excluded from the St. Louis Fine Arts Club; and, in another possible rebuke, the Wednesday Club omitted her from its American Prose Writers Series, begun that fall.[29] Confronted by this unexpected uproar, Chopin did not retreat. She refused to justify her work in the local papers, though she did publish a rather sarcastic "retraction" in a national journal in July.

But the tide of critical reviews was not stemmed, and the experience obviously left her shaken. She visited the Wisconsin lake country in October, perhaps to get some perspective on the situation, and by November had regained enough composure to write an essay for the *Post-Dispatch*. Its urbane, witty tone and the glowing headline calling her the "St. Louis Woman Who Has Won Fame in Literature" evidently soothed some hackles, and the Wednesday Club felt secure enough to include her in its special program on November 29, 1899, where some of her lyrics were performed and she read a new story, "Ti Démon."

But this tentative reentry into society did not obliterate the scandal's crushing effects. Having made what was to be her final visit to Louisiana in December, she resumed writing regularly as the new century opened. But events conspired to diminish her confidence in the acceptability of her work. In January, after a rejection by *Century*, *Atlantic* also returned "Ti Démon" as too "sombre . . . the sad note . . . too much accented."[30] And then in February, her publisher, Herbert S. Stone, returned her third collection, *A Vocation and a Voice*, with no explanation. Given their positive record of publishing potentially controversial material, the decision likely had little to do with the reception of *The Awakening*, but Chopin could hardly know that. Her writing continued for a while that spring and two stories were accepted by *Vogue*, but her dejection seems apparent in the silence of the following sixteen months, which produced not a single new tale. A brief spurt of activity occurred in the winter of 1901–1902, and two very conventional stories appeared in *Youth's Companion* the following summer.

Privately, Chopin's life more or less resumed its accustomed patterns. She continued to be a popular hostess among her friends, doubtless retaining her good-humored charm. But her lingering sensitivity about *The Awakening* is suggested by Lelia's remark that her mother never discussed its reception with her. In 1903, Chopin moved from Morgan Street to 4232 McPherson Avenue in a newer part of St. Louis. Only 52, her health had begun to fail. She needed frequent rest and expressed to her children her desire to die first—"so that *I* will not lose any one of you." There is even a possibly apocryphal family story that she sought a religious reconciliation—that shortly before her stroke she was seen coming out of a church whose confessionals were then rather fashionable.[31]

Kate Chopin's death on August 22, 1904, left six bereaved children. They buried their mother with a Requiem Mass from the Chapel of St. Louis's New Cathedral and made her grave in Calvary Cemetery, marking it with a lilac bush, her favorite flower. For a few years, most of Chopin's work remained in print. *The Awakening* was reissued in 1906, *Bayou Folk* in 1911. Then, for nearly sixty years, except for occasional mention of her as a minor local-color writer in literary histories, silence. Her simple tombstone—

Kate Chopin

February 1851

August 1904

appeared to be her only enduring commemoration. But the fiction she had created in her brief career retained a vitality that was not to be suppressed.

2

At Fault: Fictional Debut

Kate Chopin's visit with her Natchitoches in-laws in 1887, the first since Oscar's death, must have revived many memories. When she finally acquiesced to Dr. Kolbenheyer's encouragement to write, her pen flowed first with Louisiana images. But her first two stories, under way by early 1889, had abortive fates. "Euphraisie," which perhaps contains a portrait of Oscar in the young Offdean, was laid aside unfinished. "Grande Isle," an uncompleted story of some thirty thousand words, was destroyed. Her next effort, "A Poor Girl" (May 1889), was rejected by *Home Magazine*, because of some "incident – not desirable to be handled."[1] After showing it to her friend, editor John Dillon, who evidently concurred, and then unsuccessfully submitting it to the New York *Ledger*, Chopin destroyed this story, too. In June she tried an urban setting, and *The Philadelphia Musical Journal* bought "Wiser Than a God" for five dollars. But before its December appearance, she had sold "A Point at Issue!" to the St. Louis *Post-Dispatch*. In its pages of October 27, 1889, Kate Chopin made her fictional debut.

On July 5, as she meticulously recorded in her notebook, Chopin had also begun a novel. Allowing for the production of three more stories and her first commercial translation, this project occupied her for the next ten months. Like her first two published stories and many later ones, a major motif of *At Fault* was marriage and the challenges it faced in the late nineteenth century. Her subject was not unusual. The domestic novel had for several decades made marriage the focus of intense drama. Written for women and mostly by women, involving complicated plots and invincible heroines, these novels transformed a pedestrian social arrangement into a stage for heroism. Though an avid consumer of such romances as a girl, Chopin allows only a weak character like Fanny Larimore in her first book ever to be seen "reading the latest novel of one of those prolific female writers who turn out their unwholesome intellectual sweets so tirelessly" (CW, 798). But this effort to distance her own work from such modes fails to disguise how well she had absorbed the lessons of their appeal. Many of the themes and characters in *At Fault* were obviously shaped by "those prolific female writers" of the previous decades: the incurable coquette, the virtuous widow, the rejected suitor who quickly degenerates, the deserted wife, the repentant husband; alcoholism, moral and religious dilemmas, self-sacrifice, even, at least tentatively, divorce. The last, for example, which is a dramatic focus of the novel, was a very current topic in the 1880s.[2] Between 1887 and 1891, just as Chopin was beginning to write, a notable increase of articles appeared on the subject, ranging from *The Catholic World*'s wholehearted opposition to the more open views expressed in the liberal *Arena* and the eminent Boston oracle, *The North American Review*.[3] Divorce was also becoming an acceptable subject of current fiction. William Dean Howells's *A Modern Instance* (1881) was the first major novel on the matter, and a number of romances appeared in the 1880s that introduced the notion, if only to condemn it.[4]

Unlike the treatments that preceded it, Chopin's presentation of divorce is markedly neutral. Like much other domestic fiction, her novel is structured by what Larzer Ziff calls "successive marriages"—a bad one that is trenchantly criticized followed by a conventionally successful one.[5] Chopin's complication, ending the first marriage by divorce, is compromised by later killing off the first wife. Even so, as Seyersted insists, *At Fault* is "the first American novel to treat divorce amorally,"[6] and its nonjudgmental approach was to become a hallmark of Chopin's best work.

Impatient to see her work in print, Chopin suffered only one rejection, by Belford of Chicago, before she paid Nixon-Jones Printing Company of St. Louis to print one thousand copies of *At Fault* in the summer of 1890. She then sent her book to newspapers and magazines, including, quite astutely, a copy to Howells, then an editor at *Harper's Monthly*. He did not review it, but the few, mostly local, notices that did appear were generally approving.

At Fault opens in 1885, three years after the railroad had come to Natchitoches and five years after the death of Thérèse Lafirme's husband. With the railroad came a sawmill – and David Hosmer, a serious-minded lumber merchant from St. Louis. Thérèse and Hosmer are just on the verge of romance when Hosmer's visiting sister, Melicent, unwittingly reveals that her brother had been divorced two years earlier. Despite Hosmer's explanations, Thérèse sees only moral cowardice in his actions and urges him to try again. Because he loves Thérèse, Hosmer consents, remarries Fanny (whose alcoholism appears reformed), and brings her back with him to Thérèse's plantation, Place-du-Bois. Meanwhile, in a parallel romance, Melicent, an incorrigible flirt, has been infatuating Grégoire Santien, Thérèse's undisciplined nephew.

After Fanny's arrival, Thérèse begins to have misgivings. She ponders these on a visit to her former nurse, Marie Louise, whom she futilely urges to abandon her precarious cabin on the crumbling banks of the Cane River. The very next day, after an ill-fated horseback ride, Fanny is left to wait for a buggy at the cabin of Morico. The old man has an unruly, half-breed son,

Joçint, whom Thérèse has tried to help by giving him work at the sawmill, but Joçint has continued surly and rebellious. The well-meaning Morico offers Fanny a reviving toddy; she hesitates only briefly, then gulps it down and even steals the old man's bottle on her way out.

The same night, Toussaint's Eve or Halloween, Joçint stealthily burns down the resented mill. Grégoire catches him in the act and unhesitatingly shoots him. Appalled by Grégoire's lack of remorse, Melicent departs abruptly for St. Louis, without a word to the heartsick youth. Later, the house servants learn that Grégoire has been creating havoc in Centreville, drinking, gambling, forcing blacks and whites to drink together, insulting the priest, and finally riding off shooting his pistols in the air. These disturbing events parallel Thérèse's increasing awareness of the chaos she has created at Place-du-Bois. Later, in the spring, a stranger brings the news of Grégoire's murder in a bar in Cornstalk, Texas.

Soon after, Fanny crosses the rain-swollen river to renew her whiskey supply, followed by Hosmer, repentant for having angrily threatened her. But he cannot persuade her to leave Marie Louise's cabin, where he finds her; and later, waiting for her at the ferry, he watches in horror as the point to which the little house had clung sinks into the raging river. Hosmer leaps into the churning water, but he cannot save Fanny.

A year of reflection and separation later, a chastened Thérèse and Hosmer are reunited. They are soon married. Hosmer works less; Thérèse is humbler in her efforts at reform. Even Melicent writes that she means to become more intellectual and to travel in the West. The happy couple are left alone by the narrator, murmuring sweet nothings on the porch in the twilight.

The novel's major flaw is its melodramatic resolution, which conveniently removes the principal obstacle to true love, and which echoes if it does not imitate George W. Cable's story, "Belles Demoiselles Plantation"

(1875). Others have noted more subtle problems as well: extraneous and underdeveloped characters, diffused narrative focus, digressions, and a failure to provide clear motivations.[7] There are also achievements and hints of finer things to come. Certainly, the novel represents a major event in Chopin's career, articulating her serious concern for many pressing intellectual issues of her time even as it established the Louisiana settings that she soon learned to exploit more fully.

A primary focus of *At Fault* is the effects of social change in the post-Reconstruction South. The pervasive insecurity of new technologies and new philosophies assumes a form familiar in much contemporary fiction, the residual antagonisms between North and South. Change here is precipitated by the death of Jérôme Lafirme, a representative of the Old South, with its agricultural economy and conventional mores. The railroad closely follows that demise, heralding the intrusions of a new technological order—an event that Chopin herself had witnessed when the Texas and Pacific Railroad came to Natchitoches in 1881. More than a little autobiography perhaps appears in Chopin's portrait of Thérèse, distraught by the loss of a beloved husband, yet dutifully and ably assuming the management of a large, complicated estate, and even debating the merits of divorce in resolving romantic entanglements. Certainly Thérèse, in her orderly domain and old-fashioned house, views change as unwelcome but inevitable. When Hosmer, all business, all profit—suggesting the industrial future—offers to turn her "beloved woods" into lucrative planks, she hesitates only to bid "a tearful farewell to the silence" (CW, 744). For her, the mill and the "clean symmetry of sawed planks" come to mean a new orderliness, not so unlike the satisfying sweep of her well-cultivated fields.

For other representatives of the old order, this concession to progress is less heartening; but the novel suggests that only those who learn to accommodate to change can survive. Joçint, for example, resents "this intrusive Industry" that keeps a man in monotonous motion, destroying the very woods in which he would prefer to hunt at his leisure. A half-breed, his Indian heritage explains, in a stereotyped shorthand, both his devotion to an unspoiled wilderness and his violence. Though his immediate motives for burning the mill are vague, his gesture is symbolically apt, if ultimately futile and self-destructive. Similarly, Marie Louise typifies the loyalty of former slaves and the old Creole ways. Her refusal to move from the eroding bank epitomizes her obstinate rejection of change, which nature (as well as the plot) requires. Its anonymous, relentless forces overcome her, and she disappears from the novel unmourned and virtually unnoticed.

Though not so self-consciously stubborn as Marie Louise, Grégoire is just as doomed. The scion of undisciplined and now dispersed Southern aristocrats, he recalls another lost and degenerating way of life. Naturally indolent, vain, and soft-spoken, imperious and given to self-indulgence, Grégoire fits rather well the portrait of the Creole for which Cable had been so sharply reprimanded by New Orleanians.[8] Unlike Marie Louise, Grégoire is willing to change, and under Melicent's influence, he is temporarily regenerated. Melicent's affection is only superficial, however, and she proves a mockery not only of the "new woman" of the North but as a model of substantive social change as well. When she withdraws her fickle love, Grégoire reverts to uncontrolled violence, eventually dying in a vehement defense of a meaningless, aristocratic heritage.

This turbulent clash of two cultures—the agricultural South of the past and the industrialized, urban North of the future—is accented throughout the novel. The double setting, which Chopin uses so frequently and effectively in stories like "Beyond the Bayou" and later in *The Awakening*, defines these contrasts. Place-du-Bois and its environs move slowly, still more a part of nature than of civilization. Change is barely evident, announced only in the hewn logs drifting in quiet bayous, the glittery rail slicing the deep cut fringed with new growths of pine. In contrast, the St. Louis Hosmer enters to reclaim Fanny is full of "the push and jostle of the multitude." As Emily Toth has observed, Chopin's use of her native city to represent the mercantile values of modern life is characteristic.[9] Hosmer's return coincides with the St. Louis Exposition, a bustling fall showplace of technology and progress. Even his old neighborhood is altered: a former vacant lot, once the site of summer baseball, has become a crowded "row of brand new pressed-brick 'flats'" (CW, 776). Change and motion, crowds and surfaces, are the mark of modernity.

The inhabitants of these two cultures are likewise diverse. Fanny's friends, for example, Belle Worthington and Lou Dawson, are "finished and professional time-killers," women whose husbands' wealth and indifference have propelled them into the elegant leisure of matinees, elaborate toilets, expensive clothes, and clandestine tête-à-têtes with attentive men like Bert Rodney.

In contrast to Fanny's friends are Thérèse's, the Duplans. Quaint and old-fashioned in dress and manners, they talk mostly of crops and poultry and are backward enough to fail to see the Negro as an "interesting or suitable theme" of polite conversation. They retain a certain dignity and self-confidence, though, which the ill-matched Worthingtons lack. Beside them, the expansive, affected Belle and her reclusive husband, Lorenzo, seem vulgar and disconnected. Even their daughters reflect their divergences. Ninette Duplan, for example, is far more agreeable, with her spontaneity and eagerness for adventure, than the Worthington's pitiful Lucilla, intent on her religious devotions and the unchanging security of the convent. Though the Worthingtons' visit to

Louisiana is imperfectly integrated into the narrative, it does serve, if simplistically, to emphasize the differences between the modern, city couple and the old, rural order. Chopin's sympathies are clear: the vulgarity of the St. Louisans may be the future, but the grace of the Louisianians is a casualty to be regretted.

This suggestive contrast of North and South deepens in the two main characters to include broader sexual and moral issues. Even more than Melicent, Hosmer embodies the Northern intruder, a Southern image of Yankee alienation and its consequences. Obsessed with the abstractions of profit, he little grasps the gracious communal life over which Thérèse presides. Like Howells's young Silas Lapham or Bartley Hubbard, his absorption with getting has shriveled his emotions and distorted his judgment of others, estranging him from his first wife. In some ways he differs little from the expansively empty Jack Dawson, the husband of Fanny's friend, Lou. A contemporary frontiersman, Jack is a traveling salesman, more interested in conspicuous consumption and pursuing Western profits than in his relationship with his wife —who pursues sexual adventures at home. In such characters, Chopin reiterates a concern expressed in American letters as early as 1821: the American male's preoccupation with business and the detrimental effects on heterosexual relationships.[10]

As Tony Tanner eloquently testifies, marriage is both the major symbol and the primary casualty of the changes wrought on nineteenth-century society and family life.[11] Henry James, one of the period's most sensitive observers, saw the problem in terms of "an abyss of inequality." Two very different, habitual realms created two very different types of human beings—women absorbed in domestic life and emotions, men caught up in the logically relentless struggle to dominate capital.[12] Marriage was but a thin, institutional strand across that abyss. This crisis, however, as James's fiction amply demonstrates, also encompasses the problem of achieving integrity in a world that substitutes money and social success for morality and authentic relationships. The "marriage problem," then, was at root a question of the ability to distinguish the true from the false, the right from the wrong, the tawdry and superficial from the real and the genuinely individual. As a critique of the social institutions encouraging this blurred morality, the debate included the question of how to balance social needs against the rights of the individual. Such matters are at the heart of Chopin's first novel and of much of her subsequent fiction. In *At Fault*, marriage and divorce effectively dramatize the function of responsibility in achieving both selfhood and a healthy social order, and its central conflict derives from the uncertain boundaries between these dual claims.

Thérèse Lafirme, the principal focus of this dilemma, is from the outset a figure of order and tradition. Both her Southern culture and Catholic religion, with strong traditions of social responsibility and hierarchy, set her apart from the mainstream of American individualism. For Thérèse, morality is defined by the inviolability of contracts and the obligations they impose on human relationships. The whole of Part One illustrates her admirably successful attempts to secure this moral order by fulfilling her responsibilities as chatelaine. In her efforts to give Joçint productive work or Grégoire a position of responsible service, or to loosen up Hosmer's single-minded seriousness and restore his broken past, Thérèse is not simply a busybody. Instead, as the narrator reminds us, she is willing to make personal sacrifices in order to help others to do what she sees as right, which, for her, inevitably involves obligation to others (CW, 754). Thus, her primary concern in Hosmer's divorce is for the damaged social contract. In her eyes, Hosmer has, at best, unintentionally "act[ed] the part of a cruel egotist." Her analysis is searing:

> You married a woman of weak character. You furnished her with every means to increase that weakness, and shut her out absolutely from your life and yourself from hers. You left her then as practically without moral support as you have certainly done now, in deserting her. It was the act of a coward (CW, 768–769).

Hosmer's abandonment of personal relationships that he never even tried to nourish is to Thérèse an unconscionable act: a violation of the commitment to mutual support that is the foundation, not only of marriage, but of the social structure itself.

Hosmer's explanation for his poor choice of a wife has a very defensive ring:

> I am a poor hand to analyze character: my own or another's. My reasons for doing certain things have never been quite clear to me; or I have never schooled myself to inquiry into my motives for action. I have been always thoroughly the business man. I don't make a boast of it, but I have no reason to be ashamed of the admission. Socially, I have mingled little with my fellow-beings, especially with women, whose society has had little attraction for me; perhaps, because I have never been thrown much into it, and I was nearly thirty when I first met my wife (CW, 766).

The speech is important for understanding Chopin's assessment of Hosmer's error—and the shortcomings of American male individualism generally. Dramatizing the increasingly specialized functions of male and female, Hosmer acknowledges with complacency his inability to comprehend human emotions and relationships. Neither the inner life nor society holds much interest for him. These are the province of women. He, "always thoroughly the business man," has occupied himself in the male world of figures, finance, and superficial, calculated "business connections."

Other characters readily confirm this self-analysis. Belle, with her usual command of clichés, insists he is a "feller without any more feelings than a stick" (CW, 790); Fanny's major complaint was precisely his lack of companionability; Thérèse, too, blames his initial unsociability on "an unsuspected selfishness." Hosmer's dulled emotional life represents a defection from his moral responsibility to participate fully in the human community. To achieve wholeness, Hosmer must balance emotion with reason as well as deepen his bonds with society.

Certainly Hosmer's self-division has had bad consequences. His isolation, by his own admission, has made him unable to act appropriately in society. His ironically resonant reason for joining the river excursion where he met Fanny, for example, is that he perhaps "was feeling unwell"—as indeed such an *isolato* might. Inexperienced with emotions, Hosmer believed his infatuation a proper basis for marriage, and in two weeks, he proposed. Doomed to founder, the relationship was briefly shored up by a son, but when the boy died, Hosmer withdrew further into business. When he finally noticed Fanny's drinking, it was his pretext to leave altogether. Not surprisingly, he considered his important obligations to Fanny to have been financial. He pointedly observes to Thérèse that he "never permitted my wife to want for the comforts of life during my absence"; moreover, when she sued for divorce, he doubled the alimony the courts granted (CW, 768). Hosmer's material generosity is his means of satisfying social obligations and of salving his conscience.

To Thérèse, however, neither money nor even the entirely personal satisfactions of love are a sufficient base for human responsibility and right action. The "something higher" to which she insists Hosmer answer is the commitment humans make to create a community. Thérèse carefully adds, however, that her "religion doesn't influence my reason in this"; for, although her Catholicism has kept divorce an abstraction without "reference to her own clean existence," her rejection of it as a solution rests on moral principles that she holds "to be something peculiarly one's own" (CW, 764; 766). For her, and perhaps for Chopin as well, religion, like the marriage contracts it affirms, outwardly expresses the communal commitment to order that Thérèse has internalized. To destroy these visible moral supports about which humanity "twines herself," as Hosmer's friend Homeyer would do, is to leave humanity—as Hosmer left Fanny—"helpless and sprawling upon the earth" (CW, 792).

Thérèse's rejection of divorce, and her insistence that Hosmer can "do what is right" only in remarrying Fanny, is no mere prejudice, as Hosmer hopefully suggests, but an expression of a view of human life in which community and right order are the highest good, sometimes requiring the sacrifice of the self. Yet, coherent and attractive as her perspective is, the point of the novel, as Chopin insisted in her correction of a Natchitoches review,[13] is that it cannot adequately account for the legitimate needs of the individual. To this dilemma Chopin persistently reverts in her fiction. Thérèse's is, finally, a traditional view under serious and persuasive attack from the new, and very characteristically American, ideology of individualism. Both Hosmer's narrow view of human responsibility and Thérèse's failure to recognize her own limitations in comprehending what ultimately produces the common good are equally "at fault." Divorce may be a real and symbolic violation of the mutual human trust expressed in marriage, but once committed, the reparation of that rent may be more complex than mere humans can guess.

The novel examines this complexity both in terms of the authentic claims of individualism and the obstacle sheer human weakness presents to achieving moral integrity. Fanny typifies the latter; Hosmer, of course, represents the former. The case for individualism is originally made by Hosmer's mysteriously absent friend, Homeyer, whom Thérèse describes as "a mythical apology for your own short-comings" (CW, 746), a man whose indulgence in self-analysis and "deeper perceptions" excuses Hosmer from such activities. Arguing for individualism and iconoclasm, Homeyer sees Thérèse's interference as a violation of Hosmer's integrity, her insistence that he remarry Fanny as "the submission of a human destiny to the exacting and ignorant rule of what he termed moral conventionalities" (CW, 777). To Homeyer, social contracts are "arbitrary methods of expediency, which, when they outlive their usefulness to an advancing and exacting civilization, should be set aside" (CW, 793). Acknowledging their necessity, he insists that such supports are subject to constant alteration—"the inevitable natural adjustment" to which humans will respond with "an innate reserve force of accommodation" (CW, 793). Evolutionary change is, for him, the essence of human life. The folly of remarrying Fanny, then, resides in believing in redemption, in the possibility of revising the past at the individual's expense. In Homeyer's pessimistic and faintly Darwinian view, the "conglomerate whole" depends on certain "rights to existence: the existence of wrongs—sorrows—diseases—death" (CW, 777). Human life is the struggle for individual survival, which means holding on to one's personality against all the odds of mortality and finitude. Any redemptive acts that Homeyer might then concede must be made not through self-sacrifice—a senseless violation of personality—but as an "outcome from the capability of [Thérèse and Hosmer's] united happiness." Love and selfhood, not duty and responsibility, are Homeyer's highest goods.

One flaw in this view is the potential, which even Hosmer realizes, for using change as an excuse to avoid moral dilemmas. Hosmer painfully rejects just such avoidance as he struggles in St. Louis's Forest Park to accept the burden of his remarriage to a woman he has come to despise. But the truth that Homeyer articulates

—the irreparability of the past—is manifest in the confusion and pain his remarriage brings to Place-du-Bois. For Fanny, the damage is irreparable. A weak and silly woman, she is neither capable of self-redemption nor deserving of Hosmer's love could he provide it. The first time Hosmer was unable to love at all; the second time, knowing how, he loves someone else. Life, he discovers, is not a kaleidoscope whose colors "may fall twice into the same design" (CW, 817).

Thérèse too learns the limitations of her desire to do what is right. Thérèse's jealous pangs (when she realizes that Fanny actually cares for her husband) occasion her first misgivings about her "constant interference in the concerns of other people." She wonders if Fanny, and "her own prejudices," as she now sees them, are "worth the sacrifice which she [Thérèse] and Hosmer had made" of their own happiness (CW, 808). Seeing the suffering she has caused, she is no longer sure of her moral ground. "I don't know," she at last says to Hosmer; "I have seen myself at fault in following what seemed the only right. I feel as if there were no way to turn for the truth. Old supports appear to be giving way beneath me. They were so secure before" (CW, 872). Hosmer's response to the fact of human finitude is also Chopin's:

> [T]he truth in its entirety isn't given to man to know—such knowledge, no doubt, would be beyond human endurance. But we make a step towards it, when we learn that there is rottenness and evil in the world, masquerading as right and morality—when we learn to know the living spirit from the dead letter (CW, 872).

But his answer does not negate the powerful truth that Thérèse has championed: the bond of love and commitment by which humans support one another in the struggle to do what is right. Indeed, in the final chapter Hosmer seeks greater participation in the community of Place-du-Bois. As he tells Thérèse—rather sentimentally

—"Together, dear one, we will work it out . . . we may not find it in the end, but we will at least have tried." What is new in this commitment is the sense of humility that Melicent articulates: "It's impossible to ever come to a true knowledge of life as it is—which should be every one's aim—without studying fundamental truths and things . . . there's so much to be learned" (CW, 875). To this theme, the absence of moral certainty in human life, Chopin devoted some of her best fiction.

The acumen and courage of this first novel—its amoral treatment of divorce, its thematic complexity, its incisive view of male and female relationships, its skillful use of structural contrasts and the notable absence of sentimentality—are, however, overshadowed by its faults. The melodrama of the resolution, although it has symbolic value in sweeping away representatives of both Thérèse's and Hosmer's past (and is not altogether unrealistic for the area's topography), is essentially unsatisfying. A number of characters, for example, like Rufe Jimson and most of the Afro-Americans, though occasionally effective as narrators, tend to be diminished to local-color curiosities. More damaging, however, is the lack of convincing motivations, even for major figures. The psychological process of Thérèse's change, for instance, is not apparent—or even really necessary, once Fanny is conveniently disposed of. Other characters also lack emotional coherence or are overstated: the transformations of Hosmer and Grégoire, the unalleviated wickedness of Joçint (who murders his own dog!), the unsympathetic exaggerations of Lucilla and Belle, and even of the alcoholic Fanny. We remain unclear about just why Joçint burns the mill, why Grégoire is there that night, why Fanny would stop at Marie Louise's, why Melicent turns intellectual. It might be argued, of course, that in only half-revealing so many motivations, Chopin was simply accepting too superficially Maupassant's injunction to describe the surfaces of life. After all, he had gone so far as to suggest that "psychology should be concealed in the book, as it is in reality, under the facts of existence."[14] But even a well-intentioned flaw can mar a fiction, and *At Fault* is so marred.

If Chopin fails to convince us of the psychological depths of her characters, she is adept at making us hear and see them and their environs. Even early reviewers, for example, noted and praised the novel's use of setting and dialogue—elements that consistently distinguish Chopin's fiction.[15] The keen ear by which she enriches her characters is manifest in the novel's highly differentiated tongues—Belle's pseudosophisticated slang and Fanny's ungrammatical prose, as well as the modulations of French accents from Joçint's mutterings and Grégoire's careless inflections to the musical lilt of Marie Louise and the compound of local Afro-American dialect. Chopin's use of background and scene, such as Melicent and Grégoire's pirogue trips through the somber swamps, is also economical and vivid. And there are the evocations of Marie Louise's insecure dwelling, of Thérèse's verandas, of old Morico's rude cabin, and always the weather—Louisiana's tangible summer heat, the drizzly damp of its winters, the tropical torrents of its spring storms.

But juxtaposing the realism Chopin achieves with the melodramatic conventions she employs simply highlights the technical difficulties she faced in this first novel. Like her characters, Chopin was attempting to balance a personal vision against conventional imperatives. Intent on elucidating certain ideas and a particular view of human reality as well as creating saleable fiction, she achieved only partial success. But if this first novel is not entirely coherent, it is vivid and ambitious, articulating many of the thematic and technical concerns that shaped Chopin's career. And if this work is also seriously flawed, her efforts inaugurated a brief apprenticeship from which she rapidly learned to perfect her craft.

Other early work composed between June 1889 and January 1890, while she was writing *At Fault*, similarly suggests Chopin's attempts to be, at once, literate, political, and commercial. Her first tale, "Wiser Than a God" (June 1889), is about Paula von Stoltz, a young aspiring pianist whose cultured (if poor) family is contrasted with the Philistinish Brainards who employ her in the "banale servitude" of musical entertainment. Though the Brainards' son, George, proposes to her and Paula is momentarily tempted by the respectability and security of marriage, she decides, like de Staël's *Corinne*, to reject the social definitions of female happiness in order to devote herself to the higher integrity of her art, which is "dearer than life, than riches, even than love." Paula's choice exposes a serious conflict of values, linking prosperity and wedlock with superficiality and a lack of integrity. Though tempered by such conventions as the death of Paula's mother (as "punishment" for her attraction to George and marriage), or her dutiful, Victorian self-sacrifice in rejecting love,[16] Paula's conflict reflects Chopin's persistent probing of traditional assumptions. But despite such questioning of conventional values and the self-conscious acknowledgment of the epigraph that "to love and be wise is scarcely granted even to a god," Paula is allowed both. In a mild concluding twist, we are thus assured that Professor Max Kuntzler, her former teacher of harmony, still proffers his unpossessive love with the persistence and "dogged patience that so often wins in the end."

"A Point at Issue!" (August 1889), Chopin's first story to reach print, focuses the dilemmas of unconventionality more sharply. Eleanor Gail, like Paula, resists traditional marriage, which, as the narrator observes, "marks too often the closing period of a woman's intellectual existence." For her and Charles Faraday, a mathematics professor:

> Marriage was to be a form, that while fixing legally their relation to each other, was in no wise to touch the individuality of either; that was to be preserved intact. Each was to remain a free integral of humanity, responsible to no dominating exactions of so-called marriage laws. And the element that was to make possible such a union was trust in each other's love, honor, courtesy, tempered by the reserving clause of readiness to meet the consequences of reciprocal liberty.

As rational as this proposal may seem, it provokes a great outcry from a humorously judgmental society when it translates into the couple's separate residences. Though Chopin clearly admires such a radical equality in marriage, she refuses to ignore its complications in practice. The real challenge to this matrimonial experiment comes not from society but from the human heart, and even these two relatively enlightened souls find themselves victimized by their own emotions—namely, jealousy—and reduced to stereotypical roles. Eleanor ruefully acknowledges that "there are certain things which a woman can't philosophize about," and Charles silently interprets her admission as evidence of feminine weakness. Then, the narrator archly reminds us, he conveniently and "[w]ith man's usual inconsistency" forgets his own violent reactions. Faraday's final conviction that women, with their messy emotions, are the real obstacles to reasoned existence—the ones who actually need the external restraints of marriage—is a damning comment both on him and on the social order itself. But despite such an interesting conflict, the story's resolution is not altogether skillful, and both Chopin's tone and her portrayal of emotional crises (such as Eleanor's histrionic distress over Faraday's letter) are uncertain. The dialogue is often stiff as well, and certain characters, like the contrasting Beaton daughters, are insufficiently integrated into the action.

Still, the acceptance of these stories bolstered Chopin's self-confidence and prompted her to send her next tale, "Miss Witherwell's Mistake" (November 18, 1889), to the large national magazines, first *Harper's*, then *Scribner's*. Though it was rejected by these and eventually published in the more modest *Fashion and Fancy*, Chopin's initial optimism was perhaps justified. The story reflects an improved narrative integrity and tonal control, and it focuses some of Chopin's conflicting notions about the nature of fiction. A principal character is the elder Miss Witherwell, a delightful caricature of the "female litterateur" Chopin criticized in her first novel. Because she views fiction and life as very distinct realms, Miss Witherwell's mistake is precisely to confuse her niece's thwarted love affair with its fictionalized account; her suggested imposition of a romantic solution ("Marry them, most certainly, or let them die.") on a real problem ironically collapses the distinction between life and fiction that her unreal romances assert. And while the consequence of this mistake is to make reality resemble fiction, where all obstacles dissolve (such as the parental objections to the younger Miss Witherwell's suitor), its implications confirm Chopin's own realistic creed, which was to write "life, not fiction." Though Chopin's tentative critique of the false, mercantile values embodied in the city is somewhat weakened for the sake of an orthodox resolution, she does manipulate effectively the techniques of romance to mock its conventions. As in her novel, directing conventions (like the allegorical names) to realistic ends was her intent. Here, however, the more obvious subject of the writer and the more manageable medium of the short story allow for greater clarity and success.

The remaining work from this early period reflects Chopin's continuing experimentation with technique and with adjusting her art to her market. "With the Violins" (December 11, 1889), for example, is a patently commercial Christmas piece: sentimental, obviously didactic, and resolved with a not unexpected turn. But the story is unique in Chopin's canon for being exclusively in dialogue and distinctively German, capturing the desultory charm of children's voices. After this sketch, Chopin appears to have concentrated on her novels, *At Fault* and "Young Dr. Gosse," with the exception of a translation of Adrian Vely's "Monsieur Pierre," a melodramatic tale of love and violence.

In November, Chopin wrote "A Red Velvet Coat," which she records as having sold to *Youth's Companion* for fifteen dollars in February 1891, but which was evidently never printed and is now lost.[17] More fortunate was her next story. Despite its five different titles and fifteen submissions, "Mrs. Mobry's Reason" (January 10, 1891) was finally published in 1893. Reflecting contemporary concerns about venereal disease in its plot and themes,[18] this allusive tale also explores the negative powers of emotion and its association with music, a frequent motif of Chopin's work. As in *The Awakening*, music is the catalyst for a sensual awakening that is ultimately destructive. Naomi's madness, though hereditary and in a sense inescapable, is triggered by a desire that, like her mother before her, she has been unable to resist. When Naomi does fall in love, she—like Siegfried in Wagner's opera—is able to hear "what the birds are saying up in the trees" and the fish in the stream. But her privileged awareness, anticipated by her music and her instinctive appreciation of these secret harmonies, exacts the stern price of her sanity. The havoc her sensual responses wreak on her intellect—and her mother's guilt in not controlling her own desire—are focused in the melodramatic conclusion that, echoing Ibsen's *Ghosts*, awkwardly condemns the sexual forces to which both women have succumbed. Even so, the resonances of the story are quite rich and intimate major preoccupations in Chopin's fiction.

Like most writers' early work, Chopin's betrays flawed techniques, the marks of one still learning her craft. But, ambitious and eager for approval, writing one or two stories a month for the next two years, she rapidly improved with practice. Her techniques perhaps needed maturation, but her favorite themes and interests were already apparent: the relationships between men and women; the curious effects of love and its inevitable corollary, passion; the consequences of conventional restraints—both fictional and social—on the quest for integrity; the mysterious influences of music and nature; the shallow morality of mercantilism; and the oppositions of city and country, of society and the individual, of art and experience. What remained was for her to discover the element that would infuse life into her fiction. She found it in the bayou folk of Louisiana.

3

Bayou Folk: A Louisiana Local Colorist

Barely two weeks after Chopin finished *At Fault* she began work on a second novel, which she completed on November 27, 1890. *Young Dr. Gosse and Théo*, according to her letter to Stone and Kimball of Chicago, was prefaced with "a Parisian scene: the story proper opens ten years later and is acted in America." But we know no more of it. Chopin sent the manuscript to ten different publishers before she destroyed it sometime after 1895. Her friend William Schuyler had written tantalizingly in 1894 that it was "her very strongest work."[1]

But even though Chopin's second novel could find no home, the Louisiana stories she began writing in the spring of 1891 continued to be accepted. Like Sarah Orne Jewett, Mary E. Wilkins Freeman, Louisa Alcott, and Rose Terry Cooke, her national audience was largely created in children's magazines, like *Youth's Companion* and *Harper's Young People*. Though slanted toward juvenile interests, these were actually family journals with large circulations and discriminating editorial staffs where even an authority like *Harper's* William Dean Howells might notice a new author's work. In fact, he did; and Chopin's children later recalled his letter praising her sketch "Boulôt and Boulotte" in the December *Harper's Young People* and encouraging her to write more like it.[2]

Barely a vignette, "Boulôt and Boulotte" (September 20, 1891) contains many of the elements that came to define Chopin's art at its best. It is a very simple story: twelve-year-old Boulôt and Boulotte, "little piny-woods twins," set out one Saturday to buy new shoes, but return with their purchases in hand rather than on their feet. Confronted by their waiting brothers and sisters, bumbling Boulôt awkwardly acknowledges he hadn't thought of wearing the new shoes; but his unflustered sister witheringly remarks, "You think we go buy shoes for ruin it in de dus'? *Comment!*" Chopin actually manages to inject suspense into this meager event, confining our point of view to that of the expectant siblings and briefly, at least, withholding the specific reason for their shocked reactions. Howells must also have appreciated the sharp domestic realism of the piece and its lack of sentimentality, despite the tempting combination of children and poverty. But the most characteristic feature of the story, in terms of Chopin's early success, is its skillful, economic use of local color and dialect. The latter, which is confined to the climax, contributes both atmosphere and humor, while the distinctive setting is evoked with brief geographical allusions and unusual names for both people and things, like "picayunes" and "socoes."

This mastery of local-color effects perhaps indicates why Chopin's early stories were selling so well. Local color had been an extremely popular mode of fiction throughout the 1880s. Initiated with Bret Harte's and Mark Twain's stories of the West in the 1860s, the genre was enthusiastically taken up by writers throughout the country, eager to capitalize on the special flavors of their regions. Characterized by picturesque settings, phonetically spelled dialects, eccentric characters, sentimentality, humor, or a dash of romance, the fashion attracted writers like Jewett, Freeman, and Cooke in New England; Hamlin Garland, Alice French, Edward Eggleston, E. W. Howe, and Constance Fenimore Woolson in the Midwest; Mary Noialles Murfree, Thomas Nelson

Page, and Joel Chandler Harris in the South. Louisiana, with its rich mixture of cultures – French, Spanish, Afro-American, Native American, and Anglo-Saxon – proved uniquely fertile, counting George Washington Cable, Lafcadio Hearn, Ruth McEnery Stuart, Grace King – and Kate Chopin – among its interpreters. Cable in particular had promoted the eccentric figure of the Creole, and his novel *Bonaventure* (1887) was the first to describe the 'Cadian life along Bayou Teche.

Though Rankin suggests that Chopin resisted identification as a local colorist and vehemently objected to "the conventional groove" in fiction, she clearly learned much from these writers.[3] Particularly admiring Jewett for her "technique and nicety of construction," Chopin was equally adept at creating unassuming dramas of great intensity. She also shared Jewett's affection for French writers, especially Flaubert, Daudet, and of course, Maupassant, but their lightness of tone and careful phrasing would have been found in Cable or King as well. The poetic rhythms of stylists like Hearn, in his evocative *Chita: A Memory of Last Island* (1889), are likewise apparent, especially in her later work. And while she praised James Lane Allen's "A Kentucky Cardinal" as "a refreshing idealistic bit," her own fiction tended to the more biting realism of Mary Wilkins Freeman, whom she called "a great genius."[4] Freeman's portrayal of strong, unconventional characters and skillful use of dialect clearly influenced Chopin, though her Louisiana settings rarely lent themselves to the harsh isolation of Freeman's stories. Instead, Chopin tended to focus on more romantic situations, sharpening them with her realistic perspective and intense characterizations. Like Cable and King, Chopin could not resist the glamorous and eccentric variety of Louisiana's heterogeneous population, but quite unlike them, she insisted on writing about their present realities rather than their idealized pasts. In this respect, she had more in common with Ruth Stuart, with whom she also shared a lively sense of humor and sympathy for plain, back-country folk.

Chopin's particular slant on Louisiana was the Cane River country. Its bayous and cotton fields, 'Cadians and Creoles, Native and Afro-Americans, were the raw material of about half the stories that she wrote in 1891 —and they were the ones that sold first. Never a slow learner, Chopin in the next two years wrote only one short story set outside Louisiana, a sharp social satire that remained unpublished until 1897. That most of her early sales were to children's magazines also influenced the kind of stories she was writing. The moral tone and the relatively high incidence of youthful characters reflect Chopin's sense of her best market. However, she regularly sent stories to other journals like *Harper's* and *Century*, and the latter's acceptance of "A No-Account Creole" with a "flattering letter" and a hundred dollars in the summer of 1891 was certainly encouraging.[5] Other acceptances, by Boston's *Two Tales* and the new *Vogue*, followed, with the latter's inaugural issue in January 1893 featuring two stories, including "Desirée's Baby," destined to be her most famous tale. As for the novel, her failure to sell *Young Dr. Gosse* evidently convinced her that the genre was no longer congenial to her talents. Her success with Louisiana short stories persuaded her to continue in that vein.

By the spring of 1893, Chopin was ready to collect some of her stories into one volume. After negotiation on its contents, Houghton Mifflin, on March 24, 1894, brought out *Bayou Folk*, a collection of twenty-three tales and sketches—"faithful, spirited representations," the blurb ran, "of [the] unfamiliar characters and customs . . . of these semi-aliens."[6]

Though its contents reflect a broad range of story lengths and themes, the Louisiana settings and occasionally recurring characters give this created world a loose unity with its own peculiar logic. Whether writing about conventional romances and love triangles, echoes of the war and reconstruction, the stereotyped tangles of Afro- and Euro-American relationships, or cross-generational conflicts, Chopin frequently presents themes and situations from multiple vantages, achieving an unobtrusive internal dialogue that carries over from story to story and is characteristic of her fiction.

The most explicit such dialogue occurs in the first three stories: each deals with one of the "Santien boys," a family introduced in *At Fault*, and each presents his triangular relationship with a woman and another man. Though written over five years, their place at the head of the collection focuses the continuity Chopin seems to have perceived in her work, even as their increasing sophistication dramatizes her rapid growth as a writer.[7]

"A No-Account Creole" (January 24–February 24, 1891), which *Century* waited thirty months to publish, was really a revision of "Euphraisie" (1888) or "A Maid and Her Lovers," Chopin's first short story. The plot concerns the attraction of Wallace Offdean, a young New Orleans broker, for Euphraisie, an overseer's daughter on a run-down Red River plantation. Though Euphraisie is engaged to marry Placide Santien, a "no-account Creole," she is eventually released from her promise when Placide recognizes her love for Offdean.

Though, as Chopin herself remarked, "the thing drags lazily, I know—I hope not awkwardly," she was confident it contained "nothing irrelevant."[8] Major characters are, in fact, consistent and fully developed, while minor figures, who provide most of the humor (like Euphraisie's father Pierre or Placide's former nurse, La Chatte), are carefully integrated.

The main characters augur types to which Chopin often returned: the well-meaning, well-bred young city man; the clever, attractive girl from the parishes; and the fading Southern aristocrat. The focus of the tale is, as the earlier titles imply, Euphraisie herself, who must choose between her desires and right behavior. Characterized by ambivalence, Euphraisie, though able to manage her father and the run-down plantation, becomes passive when confronted with the moral dilemma of a relationship that does not elicit her passion. Chopin gratefully acknowledged R. W. Gilder's criticism of the tale and her consequent efforts to clarify the girl, "to convey the impression of sweetness and strength, keen sense of right, and physical charm beside"; but these elements remain imperfectly blended.

Offdean and Placide are more surely drawn. Their rivalry, which dramatizes latent sectional conflicts, also intimates Chopin's subtle denigration of Southern romanticism. Like David Hosmer, Offdean heralds the new order in the South. Not a "d——— Yankee" as Placide accuses, he has deliberately rejected "the maelstroms of sordid work and senseless pleasure in which the average American business man may be said alternately to exist, and which reduce him, naturally, to a rather ragged condition of soul." His rational moderation and refusal to squander his limited patrimony also distinguish him from Placide. The natural son of the old South, Placide epitomizes the Civil War's pernicious effects on "the best blood in the country." But while his arrogance and violence are anachronistic and self-defeating, his chivalric self-sacrifice for the woman he loves does belie his "no-account" title, even if, to our more cynical age, his grand gesture seems a bit forced. Nonetheless, Placide loses what he most values, forfeiting both land and Euphraisie to the new Southerner and retaining merely the useless pretensions of sovereignty—a Creole of no account indeed. The hollow ring of such romantic poses, despite their superficial appeal, constitutes a distinctive note in Chopin's fiction.

Two years later, Chopin turned to the eldest of old Jules Santien's sons, Hector, whose story, "In and Out of Old Natchitoches" (February 1–3, 1893), is second in the collection. Hector is remembered in *At Fault* as having run the plantation into debt after his father's death and now "idling on the New Orleans streets" (CW, 853). The nature of his idling is the pivot of a love triangle, whose elements echo those of the first story: a young woman who must discover her heart, an outsider who would rescue her, and a Santien who by his degeneracy forfeits her. Chopin skillfully withholds the revelation of Hector's damning flaw until the final scene, when a bystander, pointing him out, confides to his companion that there goes "Deroustan, the most notorious gambler in New Orleans."

It is an elegant finale to an imperfect tale—one whose characters, though vivid, are not particularly complex, and whose narrative tends to falter in its transition from Natchitoches to New Orleans. But the story remains interesting for its treatment of both rebellion and contemporary social issues. The pivotal incident (that triggers the would-be lovers' conflict and shifts the action to the city) is Alphonse Laballiere's attempted integration of Mlle. Suzanne St. Denys Godolph's school. As in *At Fault*, where Grégoire similary threatens to integrate a local bar, Chopin deals with the racial issue only indirectly. But while she pointedly exonerates Alphonse from any unorthodox mingling, her awareness of injustice is implied in the proposed violence to the child, the apparent lack of alternate education, and the mulatto family's quiet retreat after the incident. Chopin also sympathizes with Alphonse's resistance to convention. His angry—almost comic—speech about doing as he pleases "to hobnob with mulattoes, or negroes or Choctaw Indians or South Sea savages" intimates a strongly individualistic stance, which is echoed by Suzanne's later insistence that she can choose her own company—even Hector's. This defiance of social convention marks a recurring cadence in Chopin, although society often prevails. Even the mulattoes and the gambler here quietly withdraw to prevent compromising those whom they respect.

But although Hector's Santien chivalry inspires his gallant retreat, Chopin also exposes the faintly degenerate eroticism that has required his isolation from polite society:

> He held the rose by its long, hardy stem, and swept it lightly and caressingly across her forehead, along her cheek, and over her pretty mouth and chin, as a lover might have done with his lips. He noticed how the red rose left a crimson stain behind it.

With its marvelously restrained sensuality, the passage illustrates both the danger of Hector's character and Chopin's ability to create potent images of the passion that conventions vigorously repress.

Chopin's indirection with social issues and her skillful creation of suspense are both apparent in the third tale of *Bayou Folk*, "In Sabine" (November 20–22, 1893). Its focus is the youngest Santien, Grégoire, who also rescues a woman, though not from himself. Like his brothers, Grégoire

> loved women. He liked their nearness, their atmosphere; the tones of their voices and the things they said; their ways of moving and turning about; the brushing of their garments when they passed him by pleased him.

Enriched by its relationship to *At Fault*—to which it forms a kind of codicil—"In Sabine" follows Grégoire as he heads toward Texas, in flight from the pain Melicent had inflicted and en route to his death. The tale's expert rendering begins with Grégoire's solitary, unexplained appearance in the isolated wilderness of Sabine Parish and his slow recollection of the identity of his host, Bud Aiken, a "disreputable so-called 'Texan' who a year ago had run away with and married Baptiste Choupic's pretty daughter, 'Tite Reine, yonder on Bayou Pierre, in Natchitoches parish." Grégoire only gradually understands 'Tite Reine's plight as Aiken's unhappy drudge. But by confining our awareness of Grégoire's plans to save her to that of the drunken Aiken, Chopin manipulates our expectations so that we share Aiken's surprise—but not his chagrin—at learning that his wife has fled alone toward Natchitoches "on dat 'ar swif' hoss o' Mr. Sanchun's" while Grégoire is headed for Texas on Aiken's only animal.

A "big, good-looking brute," given to drinking and cards, Aiken is a remnant of the humor tradition of what is called the "old southwest," a "redneck" of the coarsest variety whose narrow egotism is as laughable as it is detestable. He is also a fine foil for Grégoire who, despite his arrogance and violence in *At Fault*, retains a clear moral superiority. Grégoire is evidently still pondering the novel's events: hesitating to murder Bud as he had not Joçint, and claiming to have sworn off whiskey "since day before yesterday, when he had made a fool of himself in Cloutierville." Apparently enlightened by his recent experience, Grégoire is redeemed by his chivalry, for Chopin a saving remnant of a declining class.

These contrasts in character are matched by parallels between 'Tite Reine and Mortimer. Both are victims—one of sex and one of race—and both transcend their traditional roles, but only a little. For 'Tite Reine, one of Chopin's spirited women, that transcendence is especially superficial. Though, unlike Euphraisie, she defiantly asserts her will in marrying Aiken, her consequent enslavement as an abused wife makes her virtually an object lesson in what happens to hardheaded, refractory young women. Less traditional is her defender Mortimer. Though any sexual overtones are carefully contained by his title, "Uncle," his compassion for Reine—and his axe—confirm his superiority to Aiken. Clearly pleased by Reine's escape, he savors relaying the bad news, saving the very best until last and addressing Aiken with Brer Rabbit servility: "Yas, Mas' Bud, but you see, Mr. Sanchun, he done cross de Sabine befo' sun-up on Buckeye." Just as a woman like Reine can desert her proper place if her husband is brute enough, so can a man like Mortimer manifest moral preeminence over "white trash" like Aiken. Both characters provide a glimpse of Chopin's social consciousness; but more radically in her critique of customary restraints, she does not yet venture.

The internal dialogue established in these introductory stories—and the self-contained world it implies—is continued more randomly in the fourth selection, which is the first of several domestic sketches involving fathers and daughters. Composed with three other short pieces (including "Boulôt and Boulotte"), "A Very Fine Fiddle" (September 13, 1891) is little more than a vignette, though rich with local detail. Young Fifine's initiative in selling her shiftless father's violin brings sudden prosperity, but at the questionable cost of her father's music. Chopin's touch here is light and skillful; the poignance of Cléophas' closing words suggests both the magnitude of his loss and the ambivalent price of material comfort.

A somewhat earlier and less successful story, "A Rude Awakening" (July 13, 1891), elaborates this basic situation of an energetic daughter trying to compensate for the incompetence of her father. But the tale's spirited figures (Aunt Minty and the worthless Sylveste) and unsentimental portrait of poverty do not redeem the awkward plot and obtrusive moralizing.

A third and more elaborate version of this motif, which also expands the political implications of poverty, occurs in the penultimate story, one of four published for the first time in *Bayou Folk*. "A Gentleman of Bayou Têche" (November 5–7, 1893) is the story of

Evariste Bonamour. Though as poor as Cléophas and Sylveste, he is not shiftless, and his motherless daughter, Martinette, seeks for him not money but respect. She will not have him mocked in a portrait which her neighbor, Aunt Dicey, insists will be insultingly captioned: "Dis heah is one dem low-down 'Cajuns o' Bayeh Têche!"

The story's democratic assertion that poverty does not abrogate one's claim to be a gentleman occurs in the context of ubiquitous class and racial prejudice. Though pointedly poorer than Mr. Hallet's black servants, Martinette is "puffed up" over her father's modeling. At the same time, Dicey and her son, Wilkins, openly disdain the Bonamours' simplicity; Wilkins's "visible reluctance and ill-disguised contempt" in serving them are clearly intensified by the fact that the Bonamours' color admits them to Hallet's table, despite their poverty and unsophistication. And Sublet, an outsider oblivious to the human realities of the situation, views the entire group with the snobbery of an aesthete looking for quaint diversion.

Though Chopin clearly faults all these perspectives, her story also achieves a self-reflexive irony that, characteristically, calls her own perspective, and thus that of her readers, into question. Most tellingly, this is her only borrowing of G. W. Cable's Têche setting, and that fact, coupled with Sublet's view of these people as merely "bits of 'local color,'" questions the appropriateness of the entire genre. Though Chopin was critical of local colorists' exploitations of their material, she herself was, as a writer, also an outsider. And though she may have been more sensitive to her subjects(s) than some, she must also have recognized herself as not greatly unlike Hallet who, though a fairly positive figure, remains patronizing—in both the best and worst senses. For Chopin, local color was a means of specifying her characters and enlarging their reality. Her consistent focus on action and personality instead of setting implies such a function. That she had second thoughts about her own exploitation of the genre—even a sensitive exploitation—seems clear. Certainly she never saw it as an end, and, indeed, she would eventually abandon it.

Still Chopin had "no objection to a commonplace theme if it be handled artistically or with originality,"[9] and she often relied on staple texts of Southern local-color fiction, especially "the wa'"—the Civil War, that is. Unlike Page or Allen or King, however, Chopin wrote relatively few stories that commented directly on the war's aftermath and even fewer that recollected antebellum days. Of those dozen or so tales, nine are included in *Bayou Folk*, her most conventional and best-selling collection. Placed fifth here, "Beyond the Bayou" (November 7, 1891) establishes Chopin's most familiar theme in these period stories: the war's devastating effects and the restorative powers of affection. In this tale, Jacqueline, or La Folle, dramatically overcomes the psychic and geographic confinement imposed by a violent childhood experience.

The rather extensive revisions of this relatively early story are instructive of Chopin's increasing skill. Though some changes, like the elimination of translations, reflect the transition from a children's magazine to an adult collection, others significantly diminish the melodrama of La Folle's "only mania" (her fear of crossing the bayou) to a simple fact. The role of the landscape is also enhanced, becoming, much as in Mary N. Murfree's fiction, an index of character as well as—more characteristically for Chopin—a structure for thematic contrasts. The bayou, for instance, is a psychological as well as a physical barrier, and crossing it marks La Folle's transition from solitude to the communal life of the plantation. She is catapulted there by her love for a child, a symbol of human continuity and community, just as war, their opposite, had initially thrust her into neurotic isolation.

La Folle's two trips "beyond the bayou" are also contrasted: as the first to save Chéri is terrifying, so the second the next morning is serenely beautiful. Chopin's revisions here intensify the soothing, sensual patterns of the landscape and eliminate the abstractions of the new morning's "green and white and blue and silvery shinings," which had been contrasted with the "interminable red" of La Folle's mad vision. In their place are concrete details and subtle physical parallels such as the confining crescent of the bayou and the "silver bow" of the river; the "big abandoned field" and "the woods that spread back into unknown regions," now displaced by a "broad stretch of velvety lawn" and a well-cultivated, aromatic flower garden. Such contrasts sympathetically dramatize the transformation of La Folle's psyche. In fact, her "exultation" and "deep content," the rewards of her freedom, are much more unambiguous than Chopin would later permit. Even so, the revised story amply demonstrates how well Chopin could handle conventional material – black women's devotion to white children, the lingering irrationality of war, or the power of love – both "artistically" and "with originality."

Two other stories in *Bayou Folk*, which similarly link war and madness and the redeeming effects of love, draw on another reconstruction motif: the return of the warrior to a changed world. The earlier and weaker of the tales, "A Wizard from Gettysburg" (May 25, 1891), was only Chopin's third short story with a Louisiana setting, and the second one she sold. Though the details of place and the central characters – a demented grandfather who wanders home at last and the lively fourteen-year-old grandson who unknowingly shelters him – are vivid enough, the plot soon lapses into a conventional postwar fantasy, the recovery of lost treasure.

A better variation on this theme occurs in "The Return of Alcibiade" (December 5–6, 1892), submitted "by request" to St. Louis *Life* for Christmas.[10] The tale entwines a double plot: an old gentleman's futile anticipation of his lost son's return years after the war, and an incipient romance between his granddaughter and the young pretender she drafts to satisfy the old man's one desire. The resolution is rather conventional, but the story has a rich blend of humor and detail. Both main characters are stock figures of Chopin's repertoire, but Fred Bartner's unexpected discovery of the charming Esmée and the agreeable confusion that his emotions and role-playing create echo the sophisticated comedy of Howells, which Chopin much admired. Bartner's transformation is neatly gauged by his contrasting responses to the weather in the opening and closing scenes. Initially, he is "sorely perplexed and annoyed," worrying about lost time, despite the pleasantly mild Southern winter morning about him. By the story's end, with the weather turned crisp and icy, the young man has become oblivious, even to the loss of "a whole blesse' day—a plumb day." The relativity of time is, in fact, a major motif. The return of Alcibiade or the beginning of love, like Christmas Day itself, marks a temporal lacuna, a special place where, as Monsieur Jean Ba dimly reflects at dinner, life resembles "a dream which clothes the grotesque and unnatural with the semblance of reality." This theme is complemented by a suggestive, often poetic prose; for example, the young couple's walk under the magnolias, crushing the violet borders and releasing sensuous perfumes, or the incantatory rhythms that link the tranquil deaths of the day and of Monsieur Jean Ba:

> As the sun dipped lower and lower in the west, its light was creeping, creeping up and illuming the still body of Monsieur Jean Ba. It lighted his waxen hands, folded so placidly in his lap; it touched his shrunken bosom. When it reached his face, another brightness had come there before it—the glory of a quiet and peaceful death.

Though gentle repetitions and subtle alliteration do not

quite control the pathos of the scene, Chopin's increasing mastery of language and its effects is apparent.

A slightly earlier reconstruction tale, "Ma'ame Pélagie" (August 27–28, 1892), was added late to *Bayou Folk* and placed just after "A Wizard from Gettysburg." It is Chopin's only explicit treatment of the popular Southern mythology of the golden days "befo' de wa'" and its consequences. Known as "Madame" though never married, Pélagie Valmêt and her sister Mam'selle Pauline have lived in poverty for thirty years beside the ruins of their once splendid mansion on the Côte Joyeuse—that strip of rich bottomland along the "coast" of the Red River, famed for its joyous prosperity. With her grand dreams of rebuilding, Pélagie is, in some ways, one of Chopin's strongest characters, ably managing a large plantation, once defying an enemy army, and loving faithfully not only her lost sweetheart Felix but also her sister. Nevertheless, as much as that of Monsieur Jean Ba or La Folle, Pélagie's world is an illusion of the past.

The conflict facing her, that of choosing between a beloved past and the present needs of a beloved sister, is skillfully expressed in the architectural imagery. Emotionally as well as physically, Pélagie has lived with her sister "in the shadow of the ruin" (an earlier title). As cramped by Pélagie's dream as they are by their tiny three-room cabin, the two women refresh themselves with memories that, especially for Pauline, are shadowy indeed. But when their niece, La Petite, brings them a whiff of an "outside and dimly known world," Pauline begins to share the girl's view of her aunts' existence as a "dream-life" and "a sin" against one's self and life. A fine dream sequence dramatizes the power of the myth La Petite challenges. In it, Pélagie relives one last time the festivities and tragedies of that decaying shell. The present realities of moonlight and bats and trumpet vines mingle poignantly with vividly remembered flames of chandeliers and war, together with the double pain of a soldier's new buttons pressed upon a breaking heart. But when the night fades, Venus, the star of love, not the romantic moon, guides Pélagie back to her sister and the present. With fictional as well as material economy, the ruin is at last turned to positive ends: the shapely wooden house Pélagie builds rests "upon a solid foundation of bricks"—the red bricks of the once glorious Valmêt mansion.

Pélagie's story is Chopin's version of the female tragedy of war—the loss of youth and beauty and love and home, all those elements that define a woman's existence far more explicitly than a man's. Léandre, the Valmêt son, has quite readily abandoned "the big plantation with all its memories and traditions" and has contentedly made a new life for himself in the city. Only the women remain behind, bereft of the things that gave their lives meaning and unable either to forge new meanings or to relinquish the memory of the old. But while Chopin portrays their plight with sympathetic understanding, she does not, like other Southern writers, prefer that lost era to the present. For Chopin, that past, for all its beauty, remains lost, and to dwell there is to deny what *is* valuable—present life. Ma'ame Pélagie grows old quickly when her dream vanishes; but life flourishes around her. The purpose of the past, Chopin insists, is to nourish the present, even at its own expense.

Chopin's adaptation of such conventional material to her own evolving purposes is also evident in stories that deal with Afro-Americans. Southern local-color fiction had, of course, created several stereotypes: ex-slaves nostalgic for the good old days, cheerful pickaninnies, loyal mammies and uncles, tragic mulattoes, and cruel villains.[11] Though Chopin only once portrayed the last of these—and then obliquely in "Desirée's Baby"—the others often appear, especially in her early work. *Bayou Folk* includes eight of the ten stories focusing on people of color written before the collection's 1894 appearance;

only two other stories, both written in 1896, ever repeat that emphasis, as Chopin had by then ceased to use Afro-Americans as central characters. While, like Alphonse in "In and Out of Old Natchitoches," she never quite overcame her racial biases, this group of stories reveals a gradual lessening of stereotypical views — and language — in favor of more realistic and sympathetic portrayals.

Predictably, Chopin's earliest effort to feature an Afro-American centrally is disappointing. "For Marse Chouchoute" (March 14, 1891) was the first of the *Bayou Folk* stories to appear in print. Its quick acceptance by *Youth's Companion* in April for thirty-five dollars, soon followed by "A Wizard from Gettysburg" and "A Rude Awakening," decidedly influenced her subsequent choice of subjects. Nevertheless, its patent sentimentality and moralistic emphases trivialize the story. Its remaining interests are peripheral: the depiction of a 'Cadian ball, an event Chopin used again in better fiction, and the changing of the town's name from "Centerville" to "Cloutierville." This latter usage throughout *Bayou Folk* indicates Chopin's lessening need to disguise the realities that had become her principal theme.

"Beyond the Bayou," written just eight months later, suggests Chopin's progress in realizing Afro-Americans, but three sketches in January 1892 are less successful. "The Bênitous' Slave" (January 7, 1892), for example, is little more than a stock, sentimental portrait of the loyal ex-slave and his kindly ex-masters. "Old Aunt Peggy" (January 8, 1892), a kind of companion piece, though placed after "Beyond the Bayou," is slighter but fresher. Old Aunt Peggy's elaborate anticipation of her much delayed death is treated with an agreeable lightness. The old woman has reached a venerable age — "a hundred and twenty-five, so she says." But the narrator then adds: "It may not be true, however. Possibly she is older." That final unexpected declaration is characteristic of Chopin, elevating a plain little sketch to a provocative comment.

"A Turkey Hunt" (January 8, 1892) intimates greater complexity, but it too lapses into a more superficial view of human behavior and of the sphinxlike young black servant, Artemise, than one might hope. The narrator, a plantation guest, is puzzled and fascinated with the eccentric ways and monosyllabic speech of the girl, "in some respects an extraordinary person," but little insight into the extraordinariness is forthcoming, and Artemise is instead reduced to a figure of humor, unfathomable and not altogether bright.

Chopin had more success, and perhaps more sympathy, with characters of mixed blood. In the South, of course, mulattoes, quadroons, octaroons, and other offspring of mixed parentage occupied an anomalous social position, considered black by whites and often resented for their color by Afro-Americans. While it was not included in *Bayou Folk* and remained unpublished,[12] "A Little Free Mulatto" (February 28, 1892) was Chopin's first attempt to address directly the problems of racial identification and segregation that recur in this collection. Its focus is the plight of little Aurélia, whose parents' pride in their mixed race prohibits her association with either "the white children up at the big-house, who would often willingly have had her join their games" or with "the little darkies who frolicked all day long as gleefully as kittens before their cabin doors." The child is at last transported to "paradise" when her family moves to "L'Isle des Mulâtres," an actual colony of "free mulattoes" along the Cane River, now known as Isle Brevelle. Though Chopin's sketch depicts the universality of racial pride and the pain of its isolation, it also implies her belief in the propriety of segregated communities. Aurélia's family, for instance, finds deep satisfaction in "an atmosphere which is native to them"; and the pointedly Afro-American dialect of their brief dialogue seems calculated to diminish their dignity at least in our eyes, if not in the happy Aurélia's.

Written just a few weeks later, "Loka" (April 9–10, 1892), Chopin's one story to feature a Native American as a central character, reflects similar racial biases. Snapped up by *Youth's Companion* for forty dollars, the tale recounts the reluctant incorporation of an abandoned half-breed Choctaw into a respectable, well-meaning 'Cadian family, the Padues. Despite its finely distinguished dialects and a good satirical bit on the charitable ladies of the Band of United Endeavor, the tale hinges on racial stereotypes. The Choctaw life Loka has escaped is virtually synonymous with dishonest and brutish behavior. Although Loka's inner struggles are given credibility and Mr. Padue insists on her humanity, Loka herself barely rises above the type of the stodgy, slow-witted Indian, the *vrai sauvage* of Madame's mutterings. What Chopin does convey effectively—and precisely what gives authenticity to Loka's conflict—is the intense attraction of a life in nature whose "sin and pain" a homesick Loka cannot quite separate from "the joy of its freedom." Loka's deliberate, leisurely recollection of that existence, unfolded against her survey of the vista from the cabin porch, artfully renders the ambivalence with which Chopin so often invests nature and characters lured by its possibilities.

Chopin seems to have found a better vehicle for her, at best, equivocal feelings about race in "Desirée's Baby" (November 24, 1892), the story on which her reputation rested until the 1950s. Placed in *Bayou Folk* between two stories about Afro-Americans ("The Bênitous' Slave" and "A Turkey Hunt"), the tale is about an abandoned girl, Desirée, who is adopted and beloved by the Valmondés. She eventually marries an impetuous young planter, Armand Aubigny. When their child is born "not white," her husband cruelly sends her away—to her death. Only later, while burning her effects and that of the child, does he discover a letter from his mother to his father: "'But, above all,' she wrote, 'night and day, I thank the good God for having so arranged our lives that our dear Armand will never know that his mother, who adores him, belongs to the race that is cursed with the brand of slavery.'"

The shock of this sentence, which, as Pattee says, "closes the story, but not for the reader,"[13] is the major source of admiration for this tale. Like the best of her mentor Maupassant's work in this mode, the ending not only inverts our expectations but seems inevitable in doing so. From the brooding atmosphere of the ironically named house, "L'Abri" (the shelter), to Armand's arrogance and his "dark, handsome face" beside his wife's gray eyes and fair skin, the groundwork is carefully laid for this reversal, offering the attentive reader a dreadful comprehension that the almost too convenient discovery of the letter stunningly confirms.

Apart from its calculated construction, "Desirée's Baby" also offers characters with mythical dimensions. Like the hero of classical tragedy, Armand is the proud man who comes to know himself too late as the source of "evil"—identified here with the "black blood" that Southern aristocrats like himself so feared in their legitimate offspring. More profound than any mere social stigma, however, that blackness becomes the mark of universal human darkness, that demonic region where "the very spirit of Satan" takes hold. Like Othello, whose plight as a dark foreigner marrying a fair woman resembles Armand's own situation, he is the victim of his emotional volatility. His passions are instant and furious: he falls in love "as if struck by a pistol shot," his passion sweeps along "like an avalanche, or like a prairie fire, or like anything that drives headlong over all obstacles." The violence of these similes is later echoed in the consumptive bonfire that destroys Armand's wife's and son's possessions as ruthlessly and vengefully as he had their persons. Recalling Ahab, another nineteenth-century rebel, Armand also proudly revolts against a God who has dared to injure *him*, the bearer of "one of the oldest and proudest [names] in Louisiana," a title whose very limits expose his folly. Like Melville's hero, Armand seeks a surrogate for his vengeance, but his "last blow at fate" —sending Desirée away without a word—recoils on himself in the destruction of what he most loves, the very beings who had briefly transformed his brooding spirit.

The tragic Desirée also implies depths beyond her narrative function. Like Desdemona, she is essentially passive, an innocent victim trapped by circumstances she hardly comprehends. A foundling herself, Desirée's identity is literally and metaphorically only what is given. Once she has become Armand's wife, an Aubigny, she can neither recover herself as a child of the Valmondés nor exist in any other dimension. The innocent maid who is rejected instead of cherished, Desirée has no place in life; she must die. Other ironic details abound: the adopted child of mysterious origins is "desired" while that of Armand's flesh is unwanted; Armand's mother believes the knowledge of her race will be concealed to good purpose; the stone pillar that first shelters and then becomes identified with Desirée—"silent, white, motionless"; the inverted imagery of Providence and Satan, or of black and white, including "LaBlanche," the quadroon maid, whose pale skin indicts both her mistress and her master.

But the element that gives the story its impact is its exploration of the powerful feelings about race and miscegenation that persist in American culture. Rooted in separatism, these fears are partly engendered by a misguided notion of innocence. Armand's pride is that of the "pure," whose tragedy lies in not learning soon enough that none of us are truly set apart, free from the blemishes we perceive in others. To act on such premises, as he does, ensures a rigorous isolation indeed: spiritual death. Of course, Chopin's association of black with Satanic evil and the discovery that the cruel villain of the piece *is*

Afro-American reveals her continuing ambivalence about race. Even so, her portrayal of the senseless destruction that arises from unexamined pride and fears comments powerfully on the ironic, wasteful nature of prejudice. This insight she explores again in "La Belle Zoraïde."

Published with its companion piece, "A Lady of Bayou St. John," in *Vogue*, "La Belle Zoraïde" (September 21, 1893) is Chopin's most sympathetic version of a stock figure in local-color fiction, the tragic mulatto.[14] Placed near the end of *Bayou Folk*, the tale draws together several of the volume's major themes: madness, triangular relationships, and racial pride and prejudice. Manna-Loulou's account of "La Belle Zoraïde," the beautiful quadroon, and her love for "le beau Mézor," a black slave, is a tragedy precipitated by Zoraïde's selfish white mistress, Madame Delarivière. As in "Desirée's Baby," the calamity issues from an irrational hatred of blackness and an egotistical, destructive desire for control. But while Zoraïde is more powerless than Desirée, she refuses to be shaped by others' definitions of herself. She is, she insists, "not white." And when her beloved Mézor, "straight as a cypress-tree and as proud looking as a king," is sold away and their child vindictively taken from her, Zoraïde withdraws into madness. Loved for her white beauty and despised for her black attachments, she will not endure the enforced split of her being. Zoraïde prefers instead her own private world with its senseless rag "piti" ("petite" or "little one") to the selfish, racist insanity around her. Her retreat, then, though tragic and limited, is nonetheless authentic self-assertion.

An unusual frame tale reasserts these themes and accents its layered, fictional self-consciousness. The highly crafted opening, for example, moves unobtrusively from an outdoor panorama to an interior, focusing on characters from the earlier companion piece. A passing boatman's sad patois song recalls to Manna-Loulou another old song and the story of Zoraïde, as she turns from the window to her mistress lying "in her sumptuous mahogany bed," waiting to be entertained by her personal Scheherazade. But just as this young madame's vanity and selfishness echo Madame Delarivière's, so Manna-Loulou's interjection about the incorrigibility of "negroes" betrays a self-consciousness beneath her subservient exterior and emphasizes the story's multiple awarenesses. Certainly the servant sees, as we do, more in the story than her mistress, who fastens sentimentally on the plight of the orphaned child. Her apparent obliviousness to the tragedy of a woman unable to love whom she chooses is echoed in her larger blindness to the personal and structural injustice that occasions such pain. Finally, Chopin's curious coda, which repeats the women's final conversation "in the soft Creole patois, whose music and charm no English words can convey," redoubles this narrative layering, calling attention not only to the fictiveness of this reality but also to its obliqueness, full of half-hidden, hardly understood messages. Such technical and thematic subtleties mark the tale as one of Chopin's best.

Though "A Lady of Bayou St. John" (August 24–25, 1893) elaborates the frame of "La Belle Zoraïde" and is *Bayou Folk*'s final piece, it is the earlier story. Its delineation of the young Madame Delisle's romanticism and her ensuing lack of self-definition recapitulates a major motif of the collection. Madame Delisle is the eternal child, her youth constituting her essential characteristic; it explains, if it does not excuse, the vanity of her hours before the mirror, her need for Manna-Loulou's bedtime stories, her blissful disregard for the issues of the war, except as it causes gloom. With her detached and déclassé French neighbor, Sépincourt, she imitates the abandoned grief of an absent soldier's wife. But when her husband's death transforms Sépincourt's amorous proposal for elopement into the commonplace of marriage, Madame Delisle hastily retreats into the more romantic alternative of faithful widowhood. More enamored of her private image of her husband than of his reality, Madame, who has no personal name, prefers to be defined by roles, thus evading the adult struggle for identity. Chopin's invention of the tragic self-assertion of "La Belle Zoraïde" thus mocks even as it eludes Madame, isolated in her romantic "isle" of dreams. Clutching her own senseless bundle of memories, she can only mirror-gaze uninterruptedly, forever. Despite her diminished life, however, "Madame still lives on Bayou St. John." By making this *Bayou Folk*'s concluding comment, Chopin thus gracefully links her fictions to a continuing and critical reality, one that she herself never fails to recollect or value.

Several stories in *Bayou Folk* describe a more jarring confrontation between fantasies and reality. In "A Visit to Avoyelles" (August 7, 1892), for example (which appeared with "Desirée's Baby" in *Vogue* as "The Lover of Mentine"), Doudouce fancies that he can rescue his former sweetheart, Mentine, from her worthless husband, Jules Trodon. But his impulsive visit to Avoyelles Parish, about a hundred miles down the Red River from Natchitoches, makes him a disillusioned witness to the impotence of sheer romanticism. Finding Mentine now "in a manner fallen," Doudouce loves her even more "fiercely, as a mother loves an afflicted child." Mentine, however, for all her poverty and premature age, is neither an afflicted child deserving Doudouce's condescending pity nor the helpless bride of his dream, but a woman who has made her choice and stands by it. And just as Doudouce loves Mentine beyond her dismal appearance, so does she love Jules, without regret. The final, poignant tableau, which at once clarifies her loyalties as well as the powerlessness of Doudouce's fantasy to change anything, creates a sharp twist of insight that is both dramatic and unforced. Only isolated dreams, like Madame's, appear to survive the realities of other people.

This theme and Chopin's skill at such subtle endings

is likewise apparent in a later, excellent story, "Madame Célestin's Divorce" (May 24–25, 1893), which first appeared in *Bayou Folk*. Similarly focusing on the conflict between the male fantasy of rescue and the mysterious reality of female attachment, the tale humorously addresses the social obstacles to divorce as the solution of bad marriages. Artfully told in a compact succession of scenes, it juxtaposes the adamant naiveté of pretty Madame Celéstin (married to a troublesome but absent husband) to the infatuation of Lawyer Paxton, who helpfully suggests divorce as a remedy. Humor and mild suspense characterize their formulaic exchanges over Madame's troubles: "You know, Judge, about that divo'ce." Madame's accounts are incremental in their seriousness: her family thinks divorce a disgrace, her confessor Père Duchéron considers it a scandal, and the bishop tells her it is a grave temptation. Madame's half-conscious dalliance with Paxton pointedly incorporates the expressive use of her broom: she carries it "gracefully" to the fence, ends their talks with "a flirt of the broom," and, at last, when she tells Paxton of Célestin's return, stands with it pressing the handle into her palm, "making deep rings . . . and looking at them critically." The broom suggests not only the pleasant domesticity about which Paxton daydreams, but Madame's identification with it and with the man whose phallic substitute it implies. Certainly Madame's broom-accented account of Célestin's return is accompanied by the "unusually rosy" glow of her pretty face—a blush that indicates one source of her husband's power.

Though Paxton's reaction to Célestin's homecoming promise "to turn ova [sic] a new leaf" is unrecorded, his surprise and dismay are skillfully elicited from us readers, who are identified from the outset with his point of view. Our defeated expectations for his successful courtship parallel his futile efforts to impose salvation on Madame, whose mysterious logic of love, like Mentine's, has not been taken into account. Both Paxton and Madame have succumbed to fantasies—he to the unconventional solution of divorce, she to the unfailing hope of a scoundrel's reform. Madame's reaffirmation of marriage thus satisfies conventional expectations. But the basic illusoriness of Célestin's reform as well as the source of its persuasiveness—Madame's weakness for men (that is, for sex)—allows Chopin a counter subtext. The social mythologies of marriage and reform, despite their power, prove here as unrealistic as less conventional inventions like divorce.

The next story in *Bayou Folk*, "Love on the Bon-Dieu" (October 3, 1891), treats the vagaries of love in terms of hesitation rather than illusion. Despite its uneven narrative, the tale develops sensitively the obstacles to romance, the social reproach and misunderstandings of poverty. Marking her first appearance in the respected *Two Tales*, in 1892, it also contains several fine portraits, including that of Lalie's gothic grandmother, "Ma'ame 'Zidore," crooning at the moon; the witty and sharp-tongued servant Tranquiline; and Père Antoine, whose practical charity unites the inarticulate lovers.

But perhaps Chopin's most artful combination of sexual politics and social prejudice occurs in her second *Two Tales* story, "At the 'Cadian Ball" (July 15–17, 1892). Set in St. James Parish, a cane-growing region a short way up the Mississippi River's "coast" from New Orleans, two interlocking love stories are adeptly woven around the occurrence of the title. Big, brown Bobinôt loves "that little Spanish vixen" Calixta, who has also attracted the attentions of Alcée Laballière, a local planter. In the contest for her favors at the ball, the simple farmer is no match for the suave gentleman planter. But when Alcée's elusive kinswoman, Clarisse, suddenly appears to summon him home, he responds like "one who awakes suddenly from a dream." The ball finally ends as a disappointed Calixta listlessly yields her hand to a grateful

Bobinôt, while Clarisse tells an ecstatic Alcée that she will marry him.

The narrative's subtle unfolding of the lovers' conflicts incorporates excellent local detail. For example, Chopin's survey of the ball – its midnight gumbo, the fiddlers and cardplayers, *le parc aux petits* for sleeping babies, the dancers and the gossipy chatter – establishes the gay communal context in which partners can be chosen. Similarly, secondary characters, like Bruce, Alcée's manservant, economically move the plot forward; and the black man's colorful monologue, which reluctantly reveals far more than he intends to the persistent Clarisse, exemplifies Chopin's mastery of a genre piece.

But it is the tale's psychological and social perception that distinguishes it. All four lovers want precisely what they cannot have, and, while three eventually achieve their desires, none, we suspect, will find much satisfaction in their accomplishments. The unpredictabilities of passion and the barriers of class complicate and unsettle the neat symmetry of the final couplings. And in an unpublished sequel, "The Storm" (see Chapter 7), Chopin confirms these expectations, even as the later story reverses society's earlier triumph over personal desire.

The ways in which class constrains female passion and the price of violating class limits are a central issue. Because she is only a simple 'Cadian, with Spanish blood to boot, Calixta enjoys an apparent freedom of self-expression, including fighting, swearing, and inviting "a breath of scandal" when she visits neighboring Assumption Parish. But while she enjoys exploiting her attractions, Calixta's frankly sexual appeal has clear bounds: she can charm Alcée, but she cannot claim him. As with 'Tite Reine earlier, her failure is the conventional punishment for any woman who dares to be too openly passionate: she is deserted by the rich hero and deemed lucky to get anyone, even stodgy Bobinôt.

But if Chopin does not sanction Calixta's reckless spirit, her criticism of the upper-class alternative is only more subtly depicted. Though Clarisse also focuses male attention, her role as Creole Lady—"Cold and kind and cruel by turn"—deftly conceals her pleasure in it. When Alcée, in a fit of passion, one day clasps her by the arms and pants "a volley of hot, blistering love-words into her face," she instantly chills him with "her calm, clear eyes" and disdainfully adjusts "the careful toilet that he had so brutally disarranged." Clarisse is the classic tease, the woman whose power—whose hope—lies in manipulation to defeat her rival for the male.

Of course, Clarisse's success also depends on Alcée's complicitous assent to the paradigms of feminine behavior. For him, Calixta is never more than a "little fling," a diversion from his troubles with nice (and other) women, and he forgets her as soon as he hears Clarisse's voice. Indeed, his gentlemanly expectations of winning a "real lady" blind him, finally, to anything but the patent illusion of his conquest.

The lower-class Bobinôt, on the other hand, lacks even the support of these mythologies. Though as jealous as Clarisse, he must rely on his own patient fidelity and the other woman's initiative to achieve his ends. Only after Calixta is abandoned, "almost ugly after the night's dissipation," does he have any chance with her, and even then because Calixta is as willing to spite Alcée for his rejection as Alcée was to requite Clarisse's coyness. Bobinôt's powerlessness also implies male fears of emasculation when the force of female sexuality is freed from its ladylike disguise. Certainly, Calixta's "business-like manner" in proposing to Bobinôt indicates her resignation from a game in which her natural assets are useless against the more respectable artifice of femininity.

But while this plot, like that of "Madame Célestin's Divorce," apparently confirms conventional models of female behavior, its costs suggest a deep ambivalence, echoed in the tale's final image. The end of the ball concludes the courtships, ending the dance figures that have left Alcée and Clarisse, Bobinôt and Calixta, together as partners. In the distance, there is the "rapid discharge of pistol-shots," a harmless signal, we are assured, that "*le bal est fini*"; but the ominous note of violence reverberates with the other disquieting events that have marked the 'Cadian ball. Placed among *Bayou Folk*'s final and best stories, "At the 'Cadian Ball" thus symbolically disturbs the uncertain realities that lie beneath these quaint local-color surfaces and exposes the hidden power of Chopin's finest art.

Bayou Folk represents Chopin's most sophisticated use of local-color themes—themes she had consciously exploited for commercial success; but it also reveals her recognition of their limits. For Chopin, the stereotypes of Southern aristocracy, of antebellum nostalgia, of Afro-American subservience and loyalty, even of romantic love, seem in her best work a bit frayed at the edges. That fraying was acceptable and even refreshing in a genre grown increasingly stale and, by the 1890s, playing itself out. But it also reflected a challenge both to fiction and to the society it describes. By insisting on the ambivalences concealed in these pious stereotypes, Chopin was actually forging her own, more Jamesian brand of realism and thus preparing the way for a more overt critique of the superficialities of human behavior.

Though Chopin later republished most of the Louisiana tales she omitted from *Bayou Folk*, others of the same period were never collected. These were largely stories from 1891, the year she was still experimenting, not yet having recognized the marketability of her Cane River material. Though the majority of these early tales are more interesting for their reflection of Chopin's interests than for their achievement, a few are very good fiction.

Chopin's experimentation with settings and fictional modes is especially evident in two stories from the spring of 1891. The earlier, "The Going Away of Liza" (April 4, 1891), was Chopin's first effort with Missouri country folk, a subject she returned to after 1894 with better results. Though sentimental and awkwardly constructed, the tale does provide us with Chopin's first heroine to leave her husband and demonstrates her ability to write the dialect of hill people as well as that of bayou folk.

More experimental and, fortunately, more anomalous, is "The Maid of Saint Philippe" (April 19, 1891), Chopin's only foray into historical fiction. Its subject is the courtship of Marianne, a young woman of a tiny French village on the east side of the Mississippi River, in 1765, the year the English took possession of the Illinois territory. Marianne refuses both her suitors, one who would bring her to the new French town, St. Louis, and the other who would return her to France and a life of material luxury. As she boldly asserts, "Marianne goes to the Cherokees! You cannot stay me; you need not try to. Hardships may await me, but let it be death rather than bondage."

The awkward, stilted language and the puppetlike characters no doubt indicate the uncongeniality of historical fiction to Chopin's talent. Having evidently attempted the genre, popular in the 1890s, at the insistence of friends, she records her difficulties in an 1896 essay. Lying awake at night devising a plot, reading volumes of history, poring "over folios depicting costumes and household utensils then in use," for "the first time in my life" taking notes, and feeling "very, very weary" at its completion, Chopin certainly "had taken pains" with the tale. But, she concludes, "the story failed to arouse enthusiasm among the editors. . . . Even my best friend declined to listen to it" (CW, 704).

But if Marianne is not credible, she is intriguing.

Peculiarly androgynous, she opts for celibacy as a way of resisting not only the subjection of marriage, but also political subordination. And though choosing the wilderness implies an ambivalent solitude as well as a narrative cliché, the decision typifies Chopin's attraction to "pure unadulterated nature" as a source and symbol of freedom.[15] As in the later "Loka," that freedom is incarnated in Native American life, perilous but fully integrated with nature, beyond the narrow strictures of the dominant society. The historical trappings tend to obscure, possibly deliberately, the impact of Marianne's choice of freedom—"her brave, strong face turned to the rising sun"—but her rebellion epitomizes Chopin's recurrent assertion that a woman's independence is a natural phenomenon, not an aberration.

Chopin develops this theme in the context of awakening sexuality in a delightful tale with a multivalent title, "A Shameful Affair" (June 5–7, 1891). To conventional society, the "shameful affair" is a stolen kiss; to Mildred Orme, it is her pleasure in it; to us, it is her half-conscious maneuvers to get it; but in a larger sense, it is also the Victorian ethos that conceals the pleasure of sexuality from women like Mildred or like Clarisse or, later, more tragically, like Edna Pontellier. Recalling Melicent in *At Fault*, Mildred is a coquette who little comprehends the consequences of her flirtations with an attractive farmhand. Adopting the role of the lady, she attains her ends with classic indirection but then is startled by her very unladylike responses. Characteristically in Chopin, a lush sensual setting evokes the unconventional, and the precipitous kiss occurs in an open field of "undulating wheat . . . like a golden sea" near the Merramec's "pure crystal," away from the society that would deny the sensual revelation in store for Mildred—the "hideous truth" that the kiss was "the most delicious thing she had known in her twenty years of life."

One of several sketches Chopin composed later that

year, "A Harbinger" (September 11, 1891) describes a similar feminine awakening in a natural setting, though from a masculine point of view. The allusive flower imagery and mythical names demonstrate the lyric affinities of Chopin's prose, which she nicely undercuts with the flat realism of the train that carries the disappointed Bruno away again. "Dr. Chevalier's Lie" (September 12, 1891) also shares this allusive distance and the absence of dialogue. According to Rankin, the story is a true one of a New Orleans physician who, called to a home because of the suicide of a prostitute, recognized the girl as the daughter of an Arkansas family he had once visited, and then had chivalrously concealed her "shameful" life.[16] Despite a studied, noncommittal tone, the object of the story's mild rebuke is not the girl or the doctor, but a fickle society.

These vignettes and some Louisiana stories were followed that autumn by an attempt at an altogether new genre for Chopin, the drama. Always an admirer of Howells's social farces, she was motivated by the New York *Herald*'s "Dramatic Contest" to write her own.[17] She did not win, but four years later the St. Louis *Mirror* did publish *An Embarrassing Position: A Comedy in One Act* (October 15–22, 1891). Though it took Chopin, atypically, a whole week to write, the plot—involving the cover-up by marriage of an indiscreet visit—is forced, and, despite their lively conversations, the characters are shallow and rather silly.

By the end of 1891, Chopin had turned almost exclusively to Louisiana settings, with good reason. Her last departure from that mode (until 1894) was tellingly hard to publish; and when "Miss McEnders" (March 7, 1892) finally appeared in 1897, it was over the pen name "La Tour." Perhaps the story's harsh treatment of St. Louis society accounts for the delay. Certainly, the contemporary "muckraking," in which several of her newspaper friends were involved, could have inspired the tale. As one of Chopin's sharpest social critiques, it mercilessly indicts hypocrisy in several varieties, from business corruption and self-righteous reform to sexual double standards. Chopin's portrait of Georgie McEnders's complacent virtue and idealism is devastating: she is "short-sighted," "very erect," and "almost too white-souled for a creature of flesh and blood." Though Georgie's initial complacency and later vindictiveness set her up rather too neatly for disillusionment, Chopin reserves sympathy for her quick courage in confirming her dressmaker's accusations about the sources of her father's wealth. Georgie's recognition of her own hypocrisy is wonderfully conveyed in her spontaneous disposal of her duplicitous fiancé's gift of "exquisite white spring blossoms" into the "wide, sooty, fire-place," an image of the wide sooty moral world where nothing (not even Miss McEnders) is really innocent.

Georgie's foil, Mlle. Salambre, though not so well developed, is her match in spirit. Her initial hypocrisy, calling herself "Mademoiselle" and denying her illegitimate child, is extenuated as the desperate response to an economic and moral system created by the McEnderses of the world. Mademoiselle's poverty forces her to maintain an illusion of virtue to satisfy the moral fastidiousness of women like Georgie and her women's club. But their high standards are made possible precisely by their idleness and wealth, which have removed them from the compromising struggles of existence, but which are founded on a dishonesty no less reprehensible than that enforced on Mademoiselle. Thus neither woman can claim the prescribed innocence; Mademoiselle cannot afford such a luxury and Georgie cannot assume its integrity. Only the male, Meredith Holt, can have it both ways, sacrificing neither his social position nor his wealthy pleasures to respectability.

This satire on the hypocritical efforts of the rich to improve the morality of the poor is consonant with

Chopin's impatience with both social judgmentalism and thoughtless idealism. In her diary entries of 1894, she rails at both, exclaiming over the moral pretensions of the "ladies & gentlemen sapping the vitality from our every day existence" and at the reformer who "does not ever realize the futility of effort."[18] For Chopin, the concrete substance of life was what mattered, and she had little time for those who cared only for its appearances or too superficially for its ideal possibilities. With the splendid success of *Bayou Folk* behind her as encouragement, she set out in the years following its publication to explore that substance with increased vigor and trenchancy.

4

A Night in Acadie: The Confidence of Success

Eighteen ninety-four was productive and busy for Kate Chopin. Continuing to write and sell stories, she was also occupied with promotional visits and readings for her new collection. That May, for example, having accepted yet another invitation to an "immensely uninteresting" gathering of society people, she confessed in her journal that "the commercial instinct" made her do it; "I want the book to succeed," she confided. In fact, the book was selling well. By June she had received "more than a hundred press notices."[1] Prestigious journals like *The Nation* were calling her stories "among the most clever and charming that have seen the light"; *Atlantic Monthly* praised her "distinctive power" and her "clearness of perception," and concluded that she was "a genuine and delightful addition to the ranks of our story-tellers."[2]

But mere acclaim did not satisfy her. She pointed out that among those notices, there were only a "very small number which show anything like a worthy critical faculty. . . . I had no idea the genuine book critic was so rare a bird."[3] A discriminating reader herself, Chopin had hoped for an audience appreciative of her achievements and critics who could see past the quaint, attractive surfaces of dialect and local color. Early on, she had recognized that the way to national recognition lay in exploiting the unique subject of the bayou country. But she also knew that the real quality of her fiction rested not in surfaces but in her ability to convey "human existence in its subtle, complex, true meaning, stripped of the veil with which ethical and conventional standards have draped it" — her injunction to midwestern writers that June.[4]

Chopin was keenly aware of the limitations of superficial art. After all, her discovery of "life, not fiction" in Maupassant had inspired her to write. The "naturalness and ease" of her local-color fiction were indeed, as the *Atlantic Monthly* editor had suspected, indicators "of power awaiting opportunity." The success of her collection gave her precisely the opportunity — confidence and an audience — that her fictional powers required.

Chopin further clarified her thoughts on the lasting qualities of fiction in a series of informal essays she wrote for St. Louis *Life* in late 1894. Writing first on Hamlin Garland's collection of essays, *Crumbling Idols* (1894), she reprimands the young writer's "clamor and bluster" in denouncing conventional art, even as she applauds his intent in rejecting artifice. Warning against undervaluing the significance of the past and insisting that "human impulses do not change," she declares that "notwithstanding Mr. Garland's opinion to the contrary, social problems, social environments, local color and the rest of it are not *of themselves* motives to insure the survival of a writer who employs them" (CW, 693). For Chopin, the universality of art — not its mutable social relevance — was the measure of its greatness; she even doubted Ibsen's survival because of his immersion in contemporary social problems.

This distrust of promoting unimproved experience as realistic art is likewise evident in her comments on *Century*'s October publication of some personal letters of Edwin Booth. She recoils from this unrevealing intrusion into Booth's privacy and reminds us that his art was his truest self-expression, not these pedestrian thoughts "wrung from him by the conventional demands of his daily life" (CW, 695). We may also read here a directive about her own self-expression.

But Chopin's distaste for unshaped reality is countered by an equal dislike of obtrusive moralizing. In her final review, she takes Émile Zola to task for his approach in *Lourdes* (1894). Though she admired his "masterly" style and "descriptive bits," she was offended by "the disagreeable fact that his design is to instruct us." Story, she avers, must be primary in fiction, and Zola has "swamped" his "beneath a mass of prosaic data, offensive and nauseous description and rampant sentimentality" (CW, 697). These were precisely the faults she had rejected in local-color fiction – the busy surfaces that obscured rather than revealed the realities she sought to render.

As these opinions suggest, Kate Chopin was quite conscious of the demands of her craft and the fiction she approved. That she took her art seriously is further confirmed by a brief private comment from the "Impressions" she began recording that summer of 1894. Meditating on her previous decade, the loss of Oscar and her mother, her return to St. Louis and the beginning of her writing career, she describes these as "ten years of my growth – my real growth."[5] And while she asserts her willingness to exchange them for her loved ones, she declares that she "cannot live through yesterday," lingering lovingly at gravesides. At forty-three, she had acquired a sense of which things fade and which endure, and she had no intention of pursuing the former.

Given such convictions, it can be no coincidence that immediately after the success of *Bayou Folk*, Chopin turned, for the first time in nearly two years, to non-Louisiana settings and to characters and themes much less conventional than those that had created the national audience she now enjoyed. Having caught the public's ear at last, Chopin apparently felt freed of the confines of local color and immediately set about to clarify the "subtle, complex, true meanings" that alone would give her art permanence. Paris, St. Louis, and the Missouri hills join New Orleans and Natchitoches as locales, and the unfamiliar settings that had initially sold her work now recede to simply an essential context of a specific reality. Recurring themes assume a new prominence: the unresolved tensions between a developing self and a rigid social code, the consequences of sexual awareness and its repressions, the nature and cost of self-assertion, the role of perception in human behavior. And while the first of these stories were to remain uncollected, their composition clearly affected Chopin's later Louisiana tales.

One index of Chopin's experimentalism is the difficulty she had in placing some of these new stories. *Century*, Chopin's usual first choice for her better work, rejected "The Story of an Hour," as did *Vogue* at first; after the success of *Bayou Folk*, *Vogue* reconsidered and purchased it for ten dollars. "Lilacs" was read by eight editors before the New Orleans *Times-Democrat* accepted it, two years after its composition. "Cavanelle" and "A Sentimental Soul" had similar difficulties; the latter was finally purchased by the *Times-Democrat* in 1895, continuing what had become a tradition of carrying a Chopin story at Christmas.[6]

Despite *Vogue*'s reluctance, "The Dream of an Hour" (as it was editorially titled) [April 19, 1894], is quite remarkable, ranking with *The Awakening* as one of Chopin's most memorable statements of female self-assertion. It was the first of her experimental tales, and Seyersted sees it as a direct response to her collection's success, an expression of "release from what she evidently felt as repression or frustration, thereby freeing forces that had lain dormant in her."[7]

"The Story of an Hour" recounts Louise Mallard's unexpected response to the reported death of her husband, Brently, in a train accident. Grieving alone in her room, she slowly recognizes that she has lost only chains:

"'Free! Body and soul free!' she kept whispering." Then when her husband suddenly reappears, the report of his death a mistake, she drops dead at the sight of him — of "heart disease," the doctors announce, "of joy that kills."

Chopin's handling of details illustrates how subtly she manages this controversial material. Louise Mallard's heart disease, for example, the key to the final ironies and ambiguities, is introduced in the first sentence, like the loaded gun of melodrama. But her illness gradually deepens in significance from a physical detail — a symptom of delicacy and a reason to break the bad news gently — to a deeply spiritual problem. The more we learn about Brently Mallard's overbearing nature and the greater his wife's relief grows, the better we understand her "heart trouble." Indeed, that "trouble" vanishes with Brently's death and returns — fatally — only when he reappears.

But Chopin also exposes Louise's complicity in Mallard's subtle oppression. Her submission to his "blind persistence" has been the guise of Love, that self-sacrificing Victorian ideal. Glorified in fiction Chopin had often decried, this love has been, for Louise and others, the primary purpose of life. But through her new perspective, she comprehends that "love, the unsolved mystery" counts for very little "in face of this possession of self-assertion which she suddenly recognized as the strongest impulse of her being!" As Chopin often insists, love is not a substitute for selfhood; indeed, selfhood is love's precondition. Such a strong and unconventional assertion of feminine independence likely explains *Century*'s rejection. Its editor, R. W. Gilder, had zealously guarded the feminine ideal of self-denying love, and was that very summer publishing editorials against women's suffrage as a threat to family and home.[8]

The setting, too, reflecting Chopin's local-color lessons, buttresses her themes. Louise stares through an "open window" at a scene which is "all aquiver with the new spring life." A renewing rain accompanies her "storm of grief," followed by "patches of blue sky." Then, explicitly "through the sounds, the scents, the color that filled the air," "it" comes "creeping out of the sky" upon her. Louise at first dutifully resists and then helplessly succumbs. The sense of physical, even sexual, release that accompanies her acquiescence to this nameless "thing" underpins a vision of freedom that Chopin characteristically affirms as a human right—as natural as generation, spring, or even death.

The transforming power of that insight is echoed in Louise's altered view of the future, whose length "only yesterday" she had dreaded, but to which she now "opened and spread her arms . . . in welcome." But it is a false vision. The habit of repression has so weakened Louise that her glimpse of freedom—her birthright—does not empower her, but leaves her unable to cope with the everyday reality to which she is abruptly restored. In her conventional marriage, the vision is truly illusory.

Chopin skillfully manipulates the point of view to intensify the final revelation and the shifting perspectives on Louise's life. "Mrs. Mallard" appears to us at first from a distance; but the focus gradually internalizes, until we are confined within her thoughts, struggling with "Louise" toward insight. As she leaves the private room of her inner self, our point of view retreats; we see her "like a goddess of Victory" as she descends the stairs, and then, as the door opens, we are identified with the unsuspecting Brently, sharing his amazement at his sister-in-law's outcry and his friend's futile effort to block his wife's view. The final sentence, giving the doctors' clinical interpretation of her death, is still more distant. That distance—and the shift it represents—is crucial. To outsiders, Louise Mallard's demise is as misunderstood as is her reaction to Brently's death. That even the respected medical profession misinterprets her collapse indicts the conventional view of female devotion and suggests that

Louise Mallard is not the only woman whose behavior has been misread.

Such shifting perspectives and the effort to balance the desire for freedom with realistic limitations also characterize Chopin's next story, "Lilacs" (May 14–16, 1894). Described to a prospective editor as one of her best,[9] it is her only tale set entirely in France. Its focus is Madame Adrienne Farival's annual visit to the convent of her childhood at lilac time. One year, however, she is turned away by the Mother Superior, who has learned that Madame is no pious widow, but "Mademoiselle," a professional singer in Paris.

The story's two very different environments afford an intriguing double view of Adrienne. At the convent, where she seeks a lost childhood innocence, she is part of a pastoral idyll, inhabiting a lush, spring garden of simplicity and generous female affection. But the shift to Paris reveals a different Adrienne, "clad in a charming negligé . . . reclining indolently in the depths of a luxurious armchair" in a lavish, disordered apartment. This is no innocent, but a petulant, extravagant sensualist, a star of the Paris theater. Each mutually complicating background reveals very different dimensions of Adrienne's sensuous and spontaneous but ultimately childish character.

By her second visit, our response to Adrienne has altered with that of the sisters. Instead of a jubilant welcome, she receives the Mother Superior's "bitter reproachful lines," made cruel by Adrienne's evident need for serenity, but undeniably deserved by her duplicity. This ambivalence is focused in the glimpse of her friend Sister Agathe's convulsive sorrow; the stern suppression of the nun's spontaneous affection is the painful inverse of Adrienne's irresponsible freedom.

Though Chopin attempts to balance the conflicting demands of discipline and freedom, she obviously distrusts the suppression of feeling. Such suppression was one reason she thought so little of religious life, even though her childhood friend Kitty Garesché had joined a religious community. A few days after she had completed "Lilacs" she described a recent convent visit, declaring that she "would rather be that dog" than a nun, since it was "a little picture of life and that what we had left was a phantasmagoria." That entry tellingly continues with Chopin's recollection of her own first experience of childbirth, concluding "It must be the pure animal sensation; nothing spiritual could be so real – so poignant."[10] But while Chopin impugned sensual repression, she also recognized the power of the opposing moral forces. Even Adrienne accepts the Mother Superior's banishment as just, if unkind. The bitter defeat of Adrienne's defiance is captured in the story's concluding gesture:

> After a short while, a lay sister came out of the door with a broom, and swept away the lilac blossoms which Adrienne had let fall upon the portico.

For Adrienne, discarding these harbingers of spring and renewal marks the end of innocence; but for the sisters, too, it signals the shutting out of human warmth and sensuous affection. Adrienne's irresponsibility will not again sully their closely guarded innocence, but neither will her reckless spirit liberate them from the rigid morality they defend at such a high cost.

Chopin's impatience with the superficial morality of much organized religion resurfaces in her next sketch, originally written in her diary.[11] "The Night Came Slowly" (July 24, 1894) juxtaposes the mysticism of the night and nature with the daytime visit of an unpleasant young evangelist. As in "Lilacs," the sensuousness of nature represents a more authentic access to God and the spirit than any arrogant human scheme. Chopin's particularly unsympathetic treatment of the "young fool" and his "Bible Class" emphasizes her insistence on a more transcendental path: "I would rather ask the stars [about Christ]," she concludes; "they have seen him."

A day or two later, Chopin developed this opposition of morality to human spontaneity in another diary sketch. After some changes, "Juanita" (July 26, 1894) eventually appeared with "The Night Came Slowly" in the short-lived, avant-garde magazine *Moods* (Philadelphia). Its focus is a five-foot-ten, two-hundred-pound country woman, whose attractiveness to men the narrator finds incomprehensible. Despite stories of Texas suitors with millions, however, Juanita chooses a poor, one-legged man. That they are married when she bears his child is unclear, but Chopin's conclusion is nonchalant: "For my part I never expected Juanita to be more respectable than a squirrel; and I don't see how any one else could have expected it." Reflecting Chopin's eye for the grotesque, as well as the picturesque, the sketch implies the curious couple's harmony with nature if not with human morality: "They go off thus to the woods together where they may love each other away from all prying eyes save those of the birds and squirrels. But what do the squirrels care!" The tonal ambivalence, like that in "Lilacs," accentuates the tension Chopin perceived between moral appearances and nature's serene reality.

That same summer Chopin began translating tales by Maupassant. By late 1895 these numbered six, and she approached a few publishers, unsuccessfully, with the idea of a collection to be called "Mad Stories."[12] She had previously translated an odd group of articles, presumably from French journals (pieces like "The Revival of Wrestling," "How to Make Mannikins," and "The Shape of the Head"), that she sold mostly to newspapers.[13] Like her critical reviews, her selections from Maupassant reflect her fictional interests. For example, several translations concern the occult, a topic that materializes in later work; and most deal with the obscurity of human passion, a major motif in all her fiction. Obsession—jealousy, sensual disgust, possession, or most often, the fear of isolation—dominates these "Mad Stories," which, despite their often lyrical style, express a pessimism that Chopin partly shared. Though tempered by her humor and irony, that pessimism increasingly suffuses her work.

Chopin's own stories continued to flow. By October, she had "ready another collection of Creole tales" which she hoped "to have published in book form after they have made their slow way through the magazines."[14] Two-thirds of the stories in *A Night in Acadie* (1897) were already complete and soon to be in print; others would be added. But the final collection is only superficially "another collection of Creole tales"; her confident experiments with settings and themes, and the lessons of her translations and essays, had left their mark. Fully half of the stories Chopin collected for *A Night in Acadie* were actually written before *Bayou Folk* appeared. Since she had deliberately overlooked them for the earlier volume, it seems probable that, in gathering these remaining Louisiana tales now, she counted on them to fill out any slightness and to balance her newer, bolder stories.

Certainly, the impression of *A Night in Acadie* is very different from that of *Bayou Folk*. Chopin's bayou world persists, but its romance and charm seem diminished, its happy endings muted. In fact, there are both fewer love stories and fewer tragic conclusions than before. Melodrama, too, has faded, implying a greater moral ambivalence than in *Bayou Folk*. But although this second collection contains some of Chopin's most distinguished work, contemporary reviewers were not very enthusiastic. *Nation* found the collection "sometimes a thought too heavy" and *Critic* believed it "marred by one or two slight and unnecessary coarsenesses." William Marion Reedy, however, observed more astutely in his *Mirror* that the collection was clearly about "the same old human nature that is old as mankind."[15]

A good bit of the collection's pre-1894 material features children prominently. For example, the earliest, "After the Winter" (December 31, 1891), resembles "Beyond the Bayou" (which preceded it by a month) in its reflections on the opposing effects of war and children. The plot occasionally strains for credibility, but Chopin effectively contrasts Monsieur Michel's isolated existence with the lush, magical advent of spring and the powerful harmony of the communal rituals of Easter. As for La Folle, a child is also the catalyst for Michel's return to the human community and his reconciliation with his painful past.

Children and flowers also combine positively in "The Lilies" (January 27–28, 1892). Little Marie Louise brings a "great bunch" of them to Mr. Billy in recompense for the crop damage done by her mother's rowdy calf, Toto. Touched by her gesture, Mr. Billy softens his bluster and is last seen in his best suit, callling apologetically on the child's impoverished mother. The story has a light touch and succeeds in its exaggerations, such as Mr. Billy "boiling with wrath," riding "up the lane on his wicked black charger" to make his accusations. Chopin also juxtaposes Mr. Billy's hard-nosed preoccupation with money and crops with Marie Louise's more refined sensibilities, while the notebook title, with its biblical allusion, "How the Lilies Work," reinforces this mild rebuke of materialistic values.

"That little vagabond Mamouche," who had loosed Toto in the first place, reappears a year later in another children's tale, about an old bachelor doctor who adopts the young scamp partly because he once loved the boy's grandmother. "Mamouche" (February 24–25, 1893) – "my fly speck" – was to have been part of *Bayou Folk* (which includes Mamouche's sister's story, "In Sabine"); but delays by *Youth's Companion*, which had bought the tale, forced Chopin to substitute "Ma'ame Pélagie" instead.[16] A pervasive humor partly redeems the sentimental premises expressed in its original title, "A Romantic

Attachment"; however, none of the characters possesses more depth than is necessary to point a moral about mischievous boys and nostalgic old men.

"A Matter of Prejudice" (June 17–18, 1893) is a bit later and a much better story about children and their elders. Its central character is Madame Carambeau, whose prejudices run to comic length:

> She detested dogs, cats, organ-grinders, white servants and children's noises. She despised Americans, Germans and all people of a different faith from her own. Anything not French had, in her opinion, little right to existence (CW, 282).

Using G. W. Cable's standard ploy, the story juxtaposes Madame's Creole provincialism, typified by her fortress-like French Quarter house, with her son's modern attitudes, mirrored by his residence in the American Garden District of New Orleans, with its white servants and open gardens. As in "Regret" later, with which it is paired in *A Night in Acadie*, a child's physical needs trigger the compassion that eventually reconciles Madame Carambeau with her estranged son. There is also an exquisite conclusion. Hearing that Henri has forbidden his little daughter to learn French, Madame retorts that she will teach her: "You see, I have no prejudices. I am not like my son. Henri was always a stubborn boy. Heaven only knows how he came by such a character!" Whether conscious irony or determined tunnel vision, the statement perfectly captures Madame Carambeau's crochety charm.

The next tale, "Azélie" (July 22–23, 1893), is the earliest of several rather elusive love stories included in *A Night in Acadie*, one of a series of tales of mid- and late 1893 that explore obsessive love, especially for remote or unattainable objects.[17] Though devoted to her worthless Popa, Azélie lacks the moral sense of other daughters in Chopin. But her deficiency only intensifies the infatuation of 'Polyte, the local plantation's store manager. Passive and essentially amoral (like the later "Juanita"), Azélie is indifferent to the overzealous attentions of the youth, who feels his love for her a degradation, but irresistible. Like other reformers, usually female, 'Polyte thinks he can "rescue her from . . . the demoralizing influences of her family and her surroundings." But Azélie won't cooperate, and instead, 'Polyte follows her blindly to the moral "graveyard" "yonda on Li'le river — w'ere Azélie." 'Polyte's attraction is perhaps closer to lust than love, given his oblivion to her moral failings (including theft) and his preoccupation with her physical proximity, but his loss of self is no less complete. Chopin's oblique approach to his obsession and her detached, bemused tone invite puzzlement at the hidden, chaotic forces at work on poor 'Polyte.

In "At Chênière Caminada" (October 21–23, 1893), physical passion is better transmuted into romance. When the painfully shy Tonie Bocaze (who reappears in *The Awakening*) hears the lovely Mlle. Claire Duvigné play the organ at Chênière Caminada, a Gulf Coast resort, he is immediately smitten. As uncultivated and instinctual as a Lawrentian hero, Tonie obeys the sudden dictates of love as naturally as those of hunger and thirst. But these mortal desires remain unsatisfied because their object is, for him, as remote as heaven itself. In fact, Tonie's passion is too literally mortal. Recalling an afternoon as Claire's hired sailor, he is "stirred by a terrible, an overmastering regret, that he had not clasped her in his arms when they were out there alone, and sprung with her into the sea." For her part, Claire artfully and willingly engages in romantic poses, including one that causes her death. But in dying she at last becomes "that celestial being whom our Lady of Lourdes had once offered to [Tonie's] immortal vision." Thus, like "A Lady of Bayou St. John," Tonie can fully indulge his romantic desires for his beloved. Claire's death thus unites what for Chopin were the twin transcendences of romance and religion. As in several later tales ("Lilacs," "Two Portraits," and "A Sentimental Soul"), this coupling deepens her presentation of the conflict between body and spirit, art and innocence.

"A Respectable Woman" (January 20, 1894) moves Chopin's fiction still closer to an open examination of desire. Offering perhaps her most ambivalent conclusion, it details the growing attraction of Mrs. Baroda for her husband's unassuming old friend, Gouvernail, another recurring character.[18] Though she at first flees temptation, and later opposes his second visit, she eventually encourages her husband to invite his friend again, enigmatically remarking that "This time I shall be very nice to him."

Despite its effect of surprise, this concluding equivocation is carefully anticipated. Indeed, one subtext here is precisely the ambiguous role of perception in behavior. Mrs. Baroda's initial displeasure provokes—and is provoked by—her unconscious and negative image of this man she has never met, an image instantly dissipated by Gouvernail's attractive reality. Acting the part of unconscious coquette, Mrs. Baroda exhausts her resources to secure his attentions and then so confuses her emotions that only flight can resolve her adolescent dubieties.

Gouvernail is no less oblique. Under the oak, talking "freely and intimately" of the past and present, he recites an "apostrophe to the night" from Whitman, a passage whose context is unmistakably erotic.[19] As his reserve falls away, he remarks his pleasure in this "little whiff of genuine life" out in the country, which life is for him clearly physical. The erotic tension is left sharply unresolved, the surfaces as calm as the Southern night itself. But the compelling conflict between respectability and desire is reiterated in other tensions, between Mr. Baroda's unconscious serenity and his wife's flustered confusion, between their evident affection and the turbulence of adulterous passion. That tension is further heightened by Gaston's eagerness for Gouvernail's return—and his own cuckolding. Delicate enough to tease our doubts as to whether Mrs. Baroda has finally overcome her desire or her respectability, the story eloquently delineates the electric communications of sexuality. And its poised withholding of judgment attests to Chopin's mastery of tone and authorial distance.

Though Chopin's next story marked her first appearance in *Atlantic Monthly*, "Tante Cat'rinette" (February 23, 1894) lacks the force and economy of "A Respectable Woman." A version of the faithful servant, Tante Cat'rinette is distinguished largely by her obstinacy and eccentric beliefs, fittingly concretized in her gothic nighttime trek across the fields to care for her former charge, Miss Kitty. That her dilemma of saving her house or serving her former mistress is resolved by the oracular voice of her old master betrays the tale's patriarchal assumptions. And while Cat'rinette's peculiarities measure Chopin's distance from earlier racial stereotypes, the convention of Afro-American loyalty remains unchallenged.

Chopin's next story, "A Dresden Lady in Dixie" (March 6, 1894), is not much better in terms of its racial stereotypes. However, its theme of self-sacrifice echoes a major chord of *A Night in Acadie.* The story is also a miniature of suspense: Mme. Valtour's cherished Dresden figurine is missing; the young 'Cadian Agapie is accused, though she vigorously protests her innocence even after the "lady" is found among her treasures. Some days later, Pa-Jeff, an aged and trusted servant, to whom the now exiled Agapie has always been kind, announces to the astonished household that he had stolen the figurine and hidden it in Agapie's box. Agapie is redeemed, and even Pa-Jeff comes to believe his story, "as firmly as those who had heard him tell it over and over for so many years."

Behind Pa-Jeff's generous act is the hackneyed notion of Afro-American loyalty to which Chopin so often returned—"She w'ite, I is black. . . . She young, I is ole, sho I is ole"—combined with the morality of the golden rule: "She good to Pa-Jeff like I her own kin an' color." But this bland material is flavored by Pa-Jeff's virtuoso performance in explaining his wicked deeds. His description of the battle between Satan and "de Sperrit" is a fine example of Chopin's mastery of the dialect set speech. "She do look mighty sassy dat day, wid 'er toe a-stickin' out, des so; an' holdin' her skirt des dat away; an' lookin' at me wid her head twis' . . . Satan he mighty powerful dat day, an' he win de fight. I kiar dat li'le trick home in my pocket." Even Pa-Jeff's conflict of conscience affirms a double awareness of respectability and desire.

Chopin also included two early sketches in *A Night in Acadie*. "Ripe Figs" was one of several short pieces written in early 1892. Of this group, the seven-hundred-word "The Mittens" (February 25, 1892) was destroyed, and "A Little Free Mulatto" (February 28, 1892) and "Croque-Mitaine" (February 27, 1892) (an undistinguished children's story revealing the French folk monster Croque-Mitaine to be only Monsieur Alcée en route to a costume ball) were never published. Eventually accepted by *Vogue*, "Ripe Figs" (February 26, 1892) is a fine lyrical sketch that captures a fragile sensuousness in a child's eagerness for the ripening of the figs—when she will visit her cousin on Bayou Lafourche. Chopin's harmonizing of her wait—and, implicitly, all human life—with the slow processes of nature gives a characteristic poetry and dimension to this simple event.

The later "Caline" (December 2, 1892), which has more plot than "Ripe Figs" but an equally fine lyric touch, was once admiringly described as an "exquisite bit of etching—a masterpiece in miniature."[20] In this evocation of a young girl's awakening and disillusionment, physical and emotional awakenings are exactly matched, and the poignant incompleteness of Caline's experience intimates the disappointment of all human desire. Disillusionment, a theme of several of Chopin's major stories that year, is given such delicate expression here that Josephine Donovan has suggested that Chopin might have had Jewett's sensitive story "The White Heron" in mind as a model.[21]

The ten remaining tales of *A Night in Acadie* were all written after the flush of *Bayou Folk*'s success and the experimentation that followed it. Many reflect Chopin's increasing self-confidence and more direct approach to her characteristic themes in a familiar setting. At the same time, contemporary, non-Louisiana tales parallel the concerns of those later incorporated into *A Night in Acadie*, particularly her increasing interest in duality and sexual repression. Accordingly, these intervening stories will also be treated here.

"Cavanelle" (July 31–August 6, 1894), her first Creole story in five months, is rich in mannered, picturesque detail. Its extensive revisions, some of which delete identifying references, and Chopin's contemporaneous composition of two other unusual personal narratives, "The Night Came Slowly" and "Juanita," indicate her experimentation not only with point of view (only nine of her sketches use first person), but also with the close translation of life into art. Certainly, Cavanelle is vividly drawn —"an innocent, delightful humbug" of a New Orleans merchant whose fractured speech patterns reveal his characteristic nervous energy. His one passion is his sister Mathilde, for the sake of whose wonderful voice—an illusion of his affection—he has devotedly scrimped. But when the young girl dies, Cavanelle immediately assumes the care of his Aunt Félicie—"a noble woman who has suffer' the mos' cruel affliction, an' deprivation, since the war." The female narrator then recognizes that Cavanelle's heroic devotion is its own end.

The narrator's ruminations and changing assessments of the little man give the tale an unusually meditative quality, as if she were turning a memory, trying to divine its meaning. The narrative is marked by her self-conscious lapses—not recalling which color streetcar she rode to Cavanelle's house, or what piece Matilde sang—as well as by digressive fantasies about the maid's voodoo practices or Cavanelle's self-indulgences after Matilde's death. Though her assessment of Cavanelle is identically phrased at the beginning and end of her account ("Cavanelle was an angel"), its meaning is deepened by these intervening reflections. The initial sense of saintliness includes, by the end, an awareness of Cavanelle's personal need for self-sacrifice, irrespective of the good consequences for his relatives. Devotion to others is Cavanelle's peculiar means of self-assertion.

The value of other-centeredness, a notion running counter to several stories of the spring and summer, also shapes Chopin's next tale, "Regret" (September 17, 1894), which specifically examines the limits and costs of self-sufficiency. Mamzelle Aurélie, never married, is near fifty when the unexpected, temporary care of four small children causes her to reevaluate her complacent solitude. Unlike the hero of Maupassant's tale of the same name, Aurélie has had no remorse, remaining unmarried simply because she has "never been in love." But if Aurélie's experience challenges her unconventional independence, the source of that challenge is also unconventional—the importance of the sensual life.

What the children reveal to Aurélie is exactly the sensual dimensions of her unrecognized loss. Their sticky fingers and moist kisses, their needs for aired nightgowns and clean feet, for mended clothes and rocking, disorient her orderly, almost abstract existence. The persistent animal imagery associated with the children further underlines Aurélie's limited comprehension of their bodiliness. "Little children are not little pigs," she learns, whose only need is food, nor can they, like chickens, be shooed into shelter at bedtime. But their physical demands have an emotional component with which Mamzelle only gradually comes to terms. And the depths of that revelation, the sensual dimension of love, leave her full of regret when the children depart.

Chopin intensifies the poignancy of Mamzelle's sorrow both in the affectionate portraits of the children's exactions and in the emotionally charged settings. Initially, Mamzelle's isolation is rather neutral, mirrored by her remote farm, which she inhabits "quite alone" except for her dog, her gun, and her religion. But the children rupture the contentment of that solitude. And the final, sudden stillness over the sad disarray left by her little guests and the evening shadows "creeping and deepening around her solitary figure" effectively dramatize her revelation. Mamzelle cries "like a man, with sobs that seemed to tear her very soul." But this recollection of her earlier masculine independence now seems woefully incomplete. An inverse of Louise Mallard, Aurélie has glimpsed a life that has revealed the insufficiency of her own. Though neither woman copes very well with the reality that remains, Aurélie's survival hints the superiority of independence.

Just two days later, Chopin again focused on the choices women face, arriving at still more acrid conclusions. "The Kiss" (September 19, 1894), a non-Louisiana story not included in *A Night in Acadie*, features the lovely and ruthless Nathalie, who, like Lily Bart in Wharton's *House of Mirth*, finds her plots to marry a rich man almost foiled by a more passionate admirer. But Nathalie is far less refined than Lily, and when she discovers that she cannot have both love and money, she readily settles for the latter. Unlike Aurélie, Nathalie foresees the loss of sensual love, but her faint regret also articulates the older woman's plight: "Well, she had Braintain and his million left. A person can't have everything in this world; and it was a little unreasonable of her to expect it."

Neither woman can combine independence and sensual satisfaction. But while Aurélie's ignorance sympathetically confirms conventional notions of female fulfillment, Nathalie's calculating violation of that code provokes condemnation. Indeed, the bitter realism of Nathalie's preference of security to romance, which invokes Maupassant, jars against the comic urbanity of its Howellsian plot. This curious hybrid underscores a subtle ambivalence about female roles, a duality that continued to shape Chopin's work.

"Ozème's Holiday" (September 23–24, 1894), placed last in *A Night in Acadie*, explores a more temporary regret and a lesser conflict. A lost vacation, rather than lost love, is the subject, but self-sacrifice, albeit unwilling, remains the theme. One of Chopin's most delightful opponents of the work ethic, Ozème often wonders "why there was not a special dispensation of providence to do away with the necessity for work. There seemed to him so much created for man's enjoyment in this world, and so little time and opportunity to profit by it." But Ozème also has a regrettably strong sense of duty. Step by evasive step, he is comically drawn into an act of charity on his annual vacation, picking cotton for some disabled black acquaintances. However, his real concern remains his reputation as a playboy. The delightful disparity between the philanthropic facts of Ozème's "broading" and his inventive tale about "campin' an' roughin' like" when he returns to Laballière's plantation subverts even as it confirms the story's moral about the supposedly superior pleasures of charity: "I tell you, it was sport, Bodé." For Ozème, sportive unconventionality remains a proper, though ironic, disguise for his dutiful morality.

Occupied in October by essays, Chopin followed them with two stories that again pick up these conflicting threads of self-assertion and social or religious convention. "A Sentimental Soul" (November 18–22, 1894) is Mlle. Fleurette, whose shy passion for one of her customers, Lacodie, occasions a moral crisis. Characteristically, Chopin unfolds the shopkeeper's affection gradually, showing her nervous attentions and slow awakening to love while coyly concealing the source of trouble: "He was the husband of another woman." As in "Lilacs," a natural longing for sensuous affection is opposed to a rigid moral scheme, embodied both in Mamzelle's intense scruples—"murder was perhaps blacker, but she was not sure"—and in her stern confessor, Father Fochelle. Mamzelle's long-repressed emotions at last find an outlet when Lacodie dies and his fat, attractive young wife quickly remarries. Though forbidden by Father Fochelle to indulge her romantic fantasies, Mamzelle longs to be Lacodie's bereaved and perfect lover. Given her childish dependence on external religious authority, choosing the sentimental role of spiritual widow has revolutionary implications: "for the first time in her life to take her conscience into her own keeping."

As with most great moral acts, this one is reflected in a small gesture; she goes to confession in a distant parish, and she does not submit her decision to the new priest's scrutiny. Her reaction is pure elation: "The sensation of walking on air was altogether delicious; she had never experienced it before." Though she has not escaped the categories of sentimental romance, Mamzelle's growth is real. Taking responsibility for her life and giving it even this very limited purpose is, after all, no small achievement. Indeed, as Chopin once rather wryly remarked of a friend who had declared that she lived for euchre: "Well—after all—something to live for—that is the main thing!"[22]

Chopin's next story, "Her Letters" (November 29, 1894), set in St. Louis and thus excluded from *A Night in Acadie*, explores the consequences of the secret adultery Mamzelle Fleurette did not have the courage to commit. Unable to destroy her four-year-old love letters, the unnamed woman of the story is as sentimental as

Mamzelle. Both her sustenance ("some god-given morsel") and a corrosive (whose every passionate word "had long ago eaten its way into her brain"), these letters substantiate a hidden, sensual life—her real life—and she prefers the memory of that life and love to the empty reality of her marriage.

Chopin's technique of gradual unfolding is especially apt here. Tantalizing us with the woman's "dread of possibilities" and her "premonition of danger" in going away, Chopin only clarifies her plight well into the story with the mention of the "dear one." The characters' anonymity deepens this sense of mystery and distance, which intensifies in the ironic contrast between our intimate perspective on the woman and the misperceptions of her character by her husband and closest friends. Chopin's skillful use of setting echoes this dual perspective: an external bleakness ("a leaden sky in which there was no gleam, no rift, no promise") set against a glowing interior, with its wood fire brightening and illumining the luxurious apartment to its furthermost corner. The repetition of this scene a year later—both of gestures and emotional conflict—dramatizes the very different consequences of the woman's secret life for herself and for her husband. Indeed, the final irony is that, even destroyed, her letters do exactly what she had feared they might. But their mortal power has in fact sprung from the weakness of the couple's love; while she has preferred her hidden life to his well-being, his "man-instinct of possession" has violated her right to that independent self. As the last of 1894's probing tales, "Her Letters" is an austere comment on the conflicts engendered by social and sexual roles, as well as perhaps an intriguing aside on Chopin's own romantic interlude in Cloutierville. Increasingly, as in this tale, the hidden self is the reality that conventions and superficial perceptions only conceal or distort. And while stories like "Ozème's Holiday" suggest the humor of such distortions, their ominous, destructive power defines a stronger current in Chopin's fiction.

In the early months of 1895, Chopin was writing about the bayou country more consistently; one reason may well be that her Louisiana stories continued to sell more rapidly than the others. Rather conventional in theme and technique, her first three that year were all collected in *A Night in Acadie* and feature a young person's encounter with death. "Odalie Misses Mass" (January 28, 1895) attempts to reverse the standard motif of black servants' devotion to white masters, but Odalie's motivations in missing a feastday Mass in order to care for her ancient black protégée, Aunt Pinky, lack credibility. Similarly, the authentic style of the old woman's senile reveries is marred by their conventional contents, though her life and its harsh ironies are given a modicum of emotional force.

"Polydore" (February 17, 1895) turns to the motif of the mischievous boy, though its relation to "Regret" — the exploration of women's need to mother — is highlighted by their proximity in the collection. A descendant of Huck Finn in his slow comprehensions, pleasure in deceit, and capacity for wholehearted repentance, Polydore tells a lie just to see "what would happen." However, the nearly fatal consequences to his beloved godmother reveal the dangers of falsehood. The moral, common in such *Youth's Companion* stories, is pointed. But Polydore's confession also transforms his dutiful relation with Mamzelle Adélaïde into a "bond of love . . . that would hold them together always." Human love, even the maternal kind, is as much a matter of understanding as of biology.

"Dead Men's Shoes" (February 21–22, 1895) also concerns a foster relationship whose strength exceeds that of blood. Challenged for his inheritance by insensitive relatives when his patron, old Gamiche, dies, Gilma Germain eventually yields it to them, unwilling to walk in "dead men's shoes." His grand gesture stretches both plot and characterizations, but Chopin's balancing of the various reactions to death, to possessions, and to others' misfortunes offers a perceptive comment on charity and self-interest.

After these fairly pedestrian tales, Chopin began "Athénaïse" (April 10–28, 1895). The second story in *A Night in Acadie*, it gathers several of the collection's most significant themes. An 1893 allusion to its subject, the marriage of Athénaïse Miché (in "In and Out of Old Natchitoches"), suggests that Chopin had the story in mind for some time. When Athénaïse returns home abruptly after only two months of marriage, her brother Montéclin helps her to flee to New Orleans. In a variation on Suzanne St. Denys Godolph's visit to the city in the earlier tale, Athénaïse arouses the interests of the sensitive Gouvernail, the very one who recited poetry to Mrs. Baroda ("A Respectable Woman"). While Gouvernail patiently awaits some response to his affection, Athénaïse discovers that she is pregnant, and without hesitation, returns to her husband, Cazeau, "her whole passionate nature" aroused for the first time, "as if by a miracle."

With its complex heroine and sophisticated critique of marriage and female sexuality, "Athénaïse" marks a major step on the way to *The Awakening*. While nineteenth-century ladies, in fiction and in real life, were expected to dislike any passionate expression, a lawful wedding ceremony was supposed to translate the virginal bride to the more respectable ecstasies of motherhood. In "Athénaïse," Chopin frankly examines this maidenly reticence as a function not only of sexual apprehension, but of the formidable nature of wedlock itself. That she links Athénaïse's sexual awakening with motherhood complicates her criticism of the institution of marriage, even as it probably eased *Atlantic Monthly*'s acceptance of this superb tale.

In fact, the sanctity of marriage is prejudiced

throughout the narrative's early sections: by Athénaïse's brother's helpful litany of legitimate motives for divorce —abuse, drunkenness, hatred; by their parents' observation about its "formation of a woman's character"; by her father's admiration for compelled obedience; and by Athénaïse's own view of it as a trap for young girls, even as she acknowledges "the futility of rebellion against a social and sacred institution." But the most damning evidence against marriage is perceived by Cazeau as he follows the reluctant Athénaïse home. By "some association of ideas," he suddenly recalls a childhood scene when his father had recaptured a runaway slave, Black Gabe. The memory leaves a hideous impression, and the parallel arouses a profound consciousness of the humiliation that masterhood involves. His own self-respect requires that he relinquish the right to compel another human being to do his will.

Gouvernail has a similar view of the freedom necessary for love, but, for him, wedlock is not the indissoluble bond that Cazeau glumly feels he and Athénaïse must make the best of. Rather, it is a spiritual affair, based only on the lovers' mutual desire, or, as one essayist had put it in 1889: "[a] true marriage is a natural concord and agreement of souls . . . the death of love is the end of marriage."[23] Gouvernail is simply waiting for "the death of love" of Athénaïse for Cazeau, so that he might propose a "true marriage" of souls. But while both he and Cazeau differently allow Athénaïse the freedom to choose their affection, she herself—as even neighbors recognize—is simply unacquainted with her own mind and cannot yet realize that freedom.

Athénaïse's immature notions of freedom are mingled with romantic illusions about marriage. Headstrong, like many of Chopin's finest heroines, she weds Cazeau without much forethought. But the romance of the prospect hardly prepares her for the reality of married life. As she complains to her brother:

> It's jus' being married that I detes' an' despise. I hate being Mrs. Cazeau, an' would want to be Athénaïse Miché again. I can't stan' to live with a man; to have him always there; his coats an' pantaloons hanging in my room; his ugly bare feet—washing them in my tub, befo' my very eyes, ugh!

Of course, what a nineteenth-century audience would not tolerate in print is clearly implied: sex, too, with its startling animality, hardly fulfills the promise of misty romantic dreams.

Later in New Orleans, restored to the irresponsible leisure of childhood, she delights in the familiar, "comforting, comfortable sense of not being married!" For Athénaïse, marriage not only represents a loss of freedom, but a loss of innocence. Her appreciation of Gouvernail's chaste attentions in contrast to Cazeau's way of loving ("passionately, rudely, offensively") underlines her romantic illusions. Indeed, Gouvernail's courtliness is only a style of hard-won restraint; his passions are as turbulent as Cazeau's and would doubtless be expressed in a similar way if Athénaïse would respond. Athénaïse's problem is that she has not recognized her own sensuality, the agreeable passion that would ameliorate the normal disillusionments of marriage: its invasions of privacy, its limitations on behavior, and for women, especially, its literal transformation of identity.

That pregnancy brings about Athénaïse's self-recognition is a double-edged insight. On the one hand, it affirms the emotional fulfillment of motherhood and suggests that biological experience must precede the acceptance of social roles. But Chopin's insistence on the sensual component of Athénaïse's change is significant. Knowledge of her pregnancy steeps her in "a wave of ecstasy," and when she thinks of Cazeau, "the first purely sensuous tremor of her life swept over her." Athénaïse's awakened sensibilities bring with them self-possession, too. As she had once thrown away the keys to Cazeau's house and its responsibilities, so now she demands money of his city merchant with "an air of partnership, almost proprietorship." At last, Athénaïse does "know her own mind" – and body. Her pregnancy has not only made her receptive to sexuality but offered her a new power that she did not, and could not, have as a maiden. Walking the streets of New Orleans full of her news, she feels "as if she had fallen heir to some magnificent inheritance" – as indeed she has, the possession of her body in its full potential.

Chopin's resolution of Athénaïse's dissatisfactions with marriage has suggested to some that the conclusion "contradict[s] the theme of escape" in the story, while others read irony and restlessness into the final scene on the Cazeaus' darkened porch.[24] But Chopin, though demonstrably aware of the limitations of marriage, was equally sensitive to the deeply satisfying pleasures of motherhood and the rich sensuality of reproduction. Only recall her own sensuous recollections of the birth of her first child. That she could combine both awarenesses in a single story attests to the complexity of her insight and the maturity of her skills.

"Athénaïse" is technically as well as thematically adept. The settings, ranging from the rural Cane River to the bustling French Quarter and the quiet nooks of New Orleans's West End, contribute unobtrusively to mood and theme. The presentation of consistent and well-developed characters also profits enormously from her earlier experiments with delayed exposition, which demands constant reevaluations of their nature. Cazeau, for example, is first seen worrying more about the pony his wife has ridden home than about her. His physical description as "tall, sinewy, swarthy, and altogether severe looking" with thick black hair "gleam[ing] like the breast of a crow" does little to soften this unsympathetic first impression, and we are well into the story before we discover that he feels Athénaïse's absence "like a dull, insistent pain." From that point, our response to Cazeau's stern exterior is much modified as he struggles with his powerful love for his willful and petulant young wife, and his dashed hopes that their days together "would be like w'at the story-books promise after the wedding." By the final scene, Cazeau's own deeply romantic nature, his blunt integrity, and his sensitivity are equally manifest. But the unfolding of Cazeau and other characters is as gradual and even misleading as the processes of self-discovery themselves.

With "Athénaïse," *A Night in Acadie* was essentially complete. Only two later works, including the title story, were incorporated into the collection. And Chopin's work throughout the remainder of 1895 reaffirms her gradual abandonment of local color even as it reflects her continued fascination with the later themes of duality and sexual repression.

The uncollected stories of the summer of 1895 focus on the mutability of emotion, a notion that is evident in a fragment of that May, "A Lady of Shifting Intentions," and central to the story "A Night in Acadie." "Two Summers and Two Souls" (July 14, 1895) is about lovers out of sync: a man's passion awakens a woman's, but only after her denials have cooled his. Though their stereotyped sexual responses (he precipitous and candid, she more languid and slow; she later emotional, and he stoic and businesslike) impart a certain starkness, the sketch pointedly reiterates Chopin's view of the profound gap between the sexes.

"The Unexpected" (July 18, 1895) reveals a similar disparity between lovers, though here the woman's passion fails first. The "hideous transformation" wrought by Randall's consumptive illness also afflicts Dorothea's formerly intense love, even as his disease reduces his passion to possessiveness. Though Randall tries to trade his fortune to secure her, Dorothea flees his stifling embrace to the free space of the countryside. In a variant of Nathalie's earlier dilemma in "The Kiss," Dorothea's choices are clarified in this contrast between nature's healthy sensuousness and Randall's feverish desires. And while Dorothea's change of heart is "unexpected," so is her rejection of the sentimental pose of self-sacrifice and the possessive love women were assumed to embrace.

"Two Portraits" (August 4, 1895) is a much bolder, more deliberate experiment in fiction. Once including a lost vignette of "The Wife," these conplementary sketches of "The Wanton" and "The Nun" were turned down by every editor Chopin approached. Even London's avant-garde *Yellow Book* and Chicago's *Chap-Book*, in whose pages Chopin longed to appear, refused the story.[25] Very French in spirit and dangerously risqué (by nineteenth-century American standards), each of the "Two Portraits" opens with an identical paragraph:

> Alberta having looked not very long into life, had not looked very far. She put out her hands to touch things that pleased her and her lips to kiss them. Her eyes were deep brown wells that were drinking, drinking impressions and treasuring them in her soul. They were mysterious eyes and love looked out of them.

Each sketch then diverges radically: the wanton Alberta, an abused child of a prostitute, grows up beautiful and rich through the use of her body, but also dangerous and capricious; the nun Alberta, lovingly reared by a holy woman, nourishes her spirit instead and grows rich in "heavenly delights," a visionary and a healer.

Though sexuality and religion both fulfill the opening's promise of beauty and tactile pleasure, the sketches' effects depend on the intricate interplay of these lives and the subtle confusions of sexual and spiritual fervor. Ironically, the story's shock lies less in the wanton's eloquent debauchery than in the nun's sensuous devotion. Her ecstatic visions are, as Helen Taylor points out, close in tone to the passages on Emma Bovary's last rites, for which Flaubert was tried for obscenity.

Oh, the dear God! Who loved her beyond the power of man to describe, to conceive . . . suffering, bleeding, dying for her. . . . Oh, if she might die for him in return! But she could only abandon herself to his mercy and his love. "Into thy hands, Oh Lord! Into thy hands!"

She pressed her lips upon the bleeding wounds and the Divine Blood transfigured her. The Virgin Mary enfolded her in her mantle. She could not describe in words the ecstasy; that taste of the Divine love which only the souls of the transplanted could endure in its awful and complete intensity. . . . For an hour she had swooned in rapture; she had lived in Christ. Oh, the beautiful visions!

As Taylor is quick to add, this commingling of sense and spirit is indigenous to Catholicism and preoccupied many nineteenth-century Europeans, but it was certainly not congenial to Protestant America.[26] Of course, Chopin's own background had, especially in the vocabulary of mysticism, sensitized her to the sexual dimension of the spiritual. "Two Portraits" examines these intimate connections of the flesh – sublimated in "holy passion" and realized in the healing power of "the touch of [Alberta's] beautiful hands" – and the spirit – twisted into caprice and greed and manifested in Alberta's menacing death threats. Such parallels echo George Sand who, in *Lélia*, explores this mingling in the persons of Pulchérie, the courtesan, and Lélia, the mystic.

Rather than alternative fates, Chopin's next three stories adopt alter egos to examine sexual sublimation. Almost as difficult to place as "Two Portraits," "Fedora" (November 19, 1895) was circulated for a little over a year before *Criterion* accepted it together with another troublesome piece, "Miss McEnders." Both appeared in the spring of 1897 over the pen name "La Tour." Though the faint disguise suggests reticence, Chopin may have been simply isolating these tales from the critical sketches appearing concurrently over her own name (see Chapter 5). Indeed, the stories may partly owe their publication to these commissioned essays.

If "Miss McEnders" risked offending some wealthy St. Louisans, "Fedora" risked transgressing Victorian propriety altogether. Fedora, with her oddly masculine name, has, like Pygmalion, found the opposite sex wanting in its approximation of her ideal – one formed, we are told, "too early in life." But Fedora's immature efforts at desexualization and the suppression of emotion eventually collapse in her sudden recognition of young Malthers's very attractive manhood.

Fedora is classically confused by her emotions, experiencing vague "uneasiness, restlessness, expectation" in his absence, and in his presence, "redoubled uneasiness . . . inward revolt, astonishment, rapture, self-contumely; a swift, fierce encounter betwixt thought and feeling." Her efforts to reject carnality are futile; libido will out. Fedora cannot resist touching Malthers's hat, or burying her face in his hanging coat, or going out herself to meet his sister at the train. The "long, penetrating kiss" she presses upon that startled young woman's mouth is simply the latest uncontrollable outbreak of repressed passion. The story's final image suggests a restoration of composure if not any deepening of her self-comprehension. Gathering up the reins of the symbolically "restive" brute, which she had insisted only she can govern, Fedora is once more in control, but the effort is palpable. For Chopin, the costs of Victorian repression are as telling as the rewards of release.

Chopin's next story, "Vagabonds" (December 1895), offers a more general version of repression, all the more interesting for being the last tale her biographers attribute to specific personal experience. The central encounter, between a male vagabond and a female storekeeper, has all the ambiance of "secret sharers," and a close reading reveals intricate patterns of relationship.[27] Unlike her relatives, the narrator does not resist her alleged kinship with this dissolute wanderer, Valcour. To the contrary. Although aloud she "call[s] him names" and mocks his mischief, she can "not help thinking that it must be good to prowl sometimes; to get close to the black night and lose oneself in its silence and mystery and sin." (Chopin vigorously canceled those last two words in the manuscript.) For Valcour, their meeting reaffirms his human connections and grants him the narrator's tacit approval. For her, Valcour brings close the allure of male adventure, sexual daring, and the unfettered exploration of the darker, more perilous dimensions of life she cannot experience. They are kin indeed.

"Vagabonds" marked Chopin's first Louisiana story in several months. However, she included neither it nor the next, the first of 1896, in *A Night in Acadie.* Perhaps "Madame Martel's Christmas Eve" (January 16–18, 1896) was also too closely autobiographical for comfort. It certainly isn't hard to see some facet of Kate Chopin in the melancholy widow, Mme. Martel, longing for her jovial husband at Christmas. Like Maupassant's "Lui" or "Suicide," both of which Chopin had translated, the tale examines a disordered mental state, one induced by Madame's morbid—and selfish—Christmas mourning. But unlike Maupassant, whose characters usually succumb to their delusions, Chopin realistically rebukes this Creole "luxury of grief." A substantial revenant startles Madame back to life, into the recognition that her living children, not her dead husband, offer the love she craves. This resolution affirms Chopin's increasingly realistic bent, away from the romanticism indigenous to local color.

The ironically titled story "The Recovery" (February 1896) likewise features the demise of illusions, this time following a physical recovery—by "one of those seeming miracles of science"—from blindness. After fifteen years of darkness, Jane, now thirty-five, is quite unprepared for the inevitable loss of youth she encounters in the mirror. Change in the inanimate world (at first apparently stable) dramatizes her transformed self-perceptions. Greeting the bronze figure on her French clock "as an old friend," she recognizes that it has assumed many shapes through the years—once "an imposing figure," later "a poor bit of art," and later still, a priceless treasure. These re-visions anticipate Jane's painful understanding of the changing shapes and possibilities that time requires.

Chopin's next story reverts to 'Cadian romance. Revised for *Century* to improve its "artistic or ethical value" (though it was still rejected), "A Night in Acadie" (March 1896) was the first in nearly a year to be included in her second collection, and it became the title story. Like other earlier work, it involves the rescue of a spirited young woman from a potentially disastrous marriage, one even worse than that of Mentine, who reappears as bedraggled and child-ridden as ever. Zaïda is for most of the story more audacious than either Calixta or 'Tite Reine—wearing her wedding dress to the ball, insistently driving the wagon (like Fedora), brazenly defying her parents, and finally rejecting her fiancé at the justice's cabin. As with Caline or Athénaïse, experience cures her naive romanticism abruptly, and she finally submits to the faithful and newly assertive Telèsphore. However, little prepares us for this turnabout. Indeed, Zaïda's chastening was evidently not part of Chopin's original intention. Her letter to *Century*'s editor suggests that she had altered the ending after an initial rejection, omitting "the marriage" (presumably between Zaïda and Telèsphore) and tempering the girl's character "by her rude experience."[28]

But if Zaïda's consistency falters at the end, the story remains remarkable for its stylistic excellences. Evident in the observations on the contrariness of the Creole pony or on the ball's various participants, the almost parodic tone is at its best in the description of Zaïda:

> How Zaïda's eyes sparkled now! . . . Her lips were a revelation, a promise; something to carry away and remember in

the night and grow hungry thinking of next day. Strictly speaking, they may not have been quite all that; but in any event, that is the way Telèsphore thought about them.

Just when the passage threatens to grow fulsome, Chopin transforms it into a parody that both admits extravagance of love and affirms the quite ordinary realities that evoke it.

A similar effect is produced in the fight between Telèsphore and André, which commences in high style:

The brute instinct that drives men at each other's throat was awake and stirring in these two. Each saw in the other a thing to be wiped out of his way—out of existence if need be. Passion and blind rage directed the blows which they dealt, and steeled the tension of muscles and clutch of fingers. They were not skillful blows, however.

As this mock-heroic battle rages, the fire blazes "cheerily," the kettle is "steaming and singing," and a collected Zaïda, having removed the lamp away from the fray, stands back to watch the murderous proceedings on her behalf without another word or gesture. This subtle mockery of the turbid male violence of dime novels and the rank sentimentality of the romances manifests Chopin's deft use of humor to control the passionate excesses she was exploring, not to mention a parodic perspective on her own 'Cadian material.

The next month, Chopin wrote two excellent stories, both featuring the urban poor. Even better than "Miss McEnders," these tales combine social criticism with acute portraiture. "A Pair of Silk Stockings" (April 1896), a small masterpiece, wastes no time on exposition:

Little Mrs. Sommers one day found herself the unexpected possessor of fifteen dollars. It seemed to her a very large amount of money, and the way in which it stuffed and bulged her worn old *porte-monnaie* gave her a feeling of importance such as she had not enjoyed for years.

The power of money to enhance self-esteem and confidence is the core of this poignant tale. Mrs. Sommers is a "little" person, presumably a widow, with at least four children, whose poverty, evidently a result of her marriage, has considerably reduced her stature in the community. But, unlike other more romantic widows, Mrs. Sommers has "no second of time to devote to the past." The grinding present absorbs all her energies and the future is too grim to contemplate.

Evidently she has acccepted her "littleness," though her intrepid spirit is manifest at bargain counter mêlées and in her rapturous calculations about buying clothes and shoes for her brood. This undaunted enthusiasm does, however, take its toll. Chopin mirrors her harried state in the broken syntax that describes her self-forgetfulness on her shopping trip:

> But that day she was a little faint and tired. She had swallowed a light luncheon – no! when she came to think of it, between getting the children fed and the place righted, and preparing herself for the shopping bout, she had actually forgotten to eat any luncheon at all!

Literally weakened by her devotion to others, Mrs. Sommers is unprepared for the real battle about to engage her: not the "breast-works of shirting and figured lawn," but the subtler struggles with self-indulgence. Her first response to the shopgirl's innocent query about buying stockings is automatically selfless. But the garments then become "serpent-like," glistening and gliding through her hands until the two "hectic blotches" on her cheeks announce her capitulation. The sensuous satisfaction of the silk as she dons her purchase stills any further rational activity. Her luxurious, youthful past and the self it defined, which she has so long resisted, finally erupts. In language that directly anticipates Edna Pontellier, Mrs. Sommers relinquishes the strenuous exercise of self-discipline and "abandon[s] herself to some mechanical impulse that directed her actions and freed her of responsibility."

The extent of Mrs. Sommers's self-neglect is evident in her amazement, as she buys new shoes, that those pretty feet and ankles "belonged to her and were a part of herself." As she succumbs to each successive temptation, her confidence expands. Her new accessories give "her a feeling of assurance, a sense of belonging to the well-dressed multitude." Her final indulgence is her most frivolous, a matinée. Attended by gaudily dressed women killing time, it aptly concludes her own venture into a world of make-believe. For despite her increased ease, Mrs. Sommers has only entered this world temporarily. Her presence in this essentially materialistic society is as gratuitous and evanescent as the matinée or her fifteen dollars. The dream ends, as it must for so many of Chopin's characters—Mrs. Mallard, Adrienne, Mlle. Aurélie, Jane. Mrs. Sommers becomes "little" once more.

In a bold technical move, Chopin shifts the perspective in the last paragraph to that of a man "with keen eyes." An interested but impersonal observer, like ourselves, he cannot penetrate "the study of her small, pale face." And any confidence in our own assessment is deliberately undermined by the last sentence:

> In truth, he saw nothing—unless he were wizard enough to detect a poignant wish, a powerful longing that the cable car would never stop anywhere, but go on and on with her forever.

That Mrs. Sommers is filled with regret is clear. But regret for what? for the self-indulgence of a day with the money of a windfall? for the dissipation of an illusion of well-being? for the impossibility of freedom? for the life she has chosen? for the hungry, clamoring children who await her? Chopin lets us guess. The changes in Mrs. Sommers possess an impenetrable interiority. But there is a profound poignance in her "powerful longing" and in the poverty that created it, burdening with guilt even so small a self-indulgence.

Chopin's consciousness of poverty's effects on selfhood is equally apparent in "Nég Créol" (April 1896), which features the eccentric Chicot, clinging to the fringes of society, grasping at both survival and human dignity. As for Tante Cat'rinette, Chicot's idiosyncrasies and illusions raise him above the stereotype of the exslave; Chicot is one of Chopin's final and most sensitive portrayals of an Afro-American. Like "little Mrs. Sommers," Chicot is insignificant in his urban world. Even in the unselective society of the French Market, he is "so black, lean, lame, and shriveled" that "one felt privileged to call him almost anything." Chicot, however, transforms his marginality into a virtue. His wildly comic religious beliefs and his inflation of the magnificent Boisduré family (both ironic consequences of his slavery) are essential to Chicot's self-respect. And even though the last remnant of the Boisdurés is, in fact, the impoverished Mlle. Aglaé (as unable to support herself as to aggrandize her servants by their association), Chicot's devotion gives his life purpose and value.

Mademoiselle's own illusions echo these fragile claims to a fragile dignity. Like Chicot, she entrenches herself in eccentricities and intolerance to affirm her selfhood. She deliberately irritates him, challenging his odd beliefs with her own showy but more conventional devotions. Mademoiselle prefers to believe that she does not need a poor black man's charity, though, of course, she does; and she needs not only the spoils of his begging and pitiful earnings, but also his attentions to her endless complaints. Chicot bears them readily, since for him they voice a just protest against her disgraceful poverty and his own humiliation.

The balance of support between these two, however, only mirrors the larger network of charity that dignifies the lives of the poor. Not only does Chicot exist on the lagniappe of the French Market vendors, but when Mademoiselle dies, the kindness of her eccentric neighbors is manifest: "Purgatory Mary" with her Lourdes water and borrowed candlesticks, the generous Irish woman Brigitte, and even the curious but respectful "street Arabs" who attend the wake. Even Chicot's refusal to pray to the negligent "Michié bon Dieu," despite the pain of Mademoiselle's loss, marks an uncompromising devotion to their failing dignity. Similarly, when the fishmonger's Italian wife remarks that one of his famous Boisdurés has died—"po', same-a like church rat"—Chicot emphatically denies any connections with *his* Boisdurés and even declines to watch the small funeral procession wend past the Market. His apparent betrayal is, of course, intense fidelity, not only to Mademoiselle, but also to his own dignity as the former servant of the unexceptionally magnificent Boisdurés.

This portrait of the struggle for self-respect among the poor recalls an earlier treatment of the same theme, "A Gentleman of Bayou Têche." But the shift from the lush Têche countryside to the urban bustle of New Orleans marks the distance between *A Night in Acadie* (of which "Nég Créol" was the latest story included) and *Bayou Folk*. In the earlier story, Evariste needs no illusions to confirm his gentlemanhood; he earns the title by his deed; only outsiders like Mr. Sublet must learn to penetrate the facade of his poverty, to see more than "local color." But for Chicot, illusions are the only substance, since no amount of generosity or service or self-sacrifice could in contemporary Euro-American eyes elevate a poor Afro-American to the dignity of gentleman. Chicot's eccentricities, even his poverty, have become his essence. His life does not reflect, but *is* local color. Evariste's quaint surfaces, when one sees them without prejudice, reveal the hidden realities of his human dignity. For Chicot those eccentric appearances are intrinsic to his selfhood. Rather than penetrate his surfaces, one must comprehend the peculiar reality of Chicot's perceptions: see how he sees, and recognize the value that vision comprehends. As for later modernists like James or Faulkner, perspective itself proves as powerful an element of fiction as any precise delineation of its contents.

Though not as incisive as "Nég Créol," Chopin's succeeding story, "Aunt Lympy's Interference" (June 1896), also explores the consequences of poverty—a consistent theme in her work throughout the first half of 1896. It also marks her final treatment of Afro-American loyalty, that quintessentially Reconstruction theme. But the spirit here is comic, not tragic; and love rather than death provides the denouement. The tale pits the appeal of Melitte's economic independence as "school-titcher" against the déclassé attractions of high society. However, the conventional outcome reaffirms Chopin's realistic insistence that society's expectations, more subtly than our own, definitely shape our behavior. Melitte's rebellion thus inadvertently accomplishes her conformity to woman's "proper" role.

Though set in Louisiana, "Aunt Lympy's Interference" was not included in *A Night in Acadie*, and the collection was complete with "Nég Créol," a fitting climax to Chopin's work as a local colorist. Her second collection was in many ways her final statement on the genre that had brought her national prominence. Chopin continued to use Louisiana settings effectively, but her dependence on them ceased. The confident experimentation following *Bayou Folk*'s success had definitively widened her range of themes and settings. The very unevenness of *A Night in Acadie*, gathering early tales excluded from her first collection together with many outstanding later stories, reflects this transition. The final effect of *A Night in Acadie* is one of increasing subtlety and reach in Chopin's talent as well as a new sense that evoking the quaintness of Louisiana was no longer her primary intent. Chopin was on a new course in her fiction, en route to an examination of human life more honest than she, or many others, had yet dared.

5

Realizations:
A Vocation and a Voice

A Night in Acadie had not been easy to place. Though Chopin had said it was ready in October 1894, Houghton Mifflin was suggesting as late as July 1895 that she postpone pressing the matter with them. Further inquiries there and to Lippincott's in March 1895 indicate that she was also by then trying to sell her translations of Maupassant. In November, she sent a collection of stories to Stone and Kimball, a new Chicago publishing house. While this may have been *A Night in Acadie*, the implied inclusion of "Lilacs" and "Three [sic] Portraits" argues that this was yet another collection, never published, called *A Vocation and a Voice.*[1]

Borrowing the title of an 1896 story, the collection is first named in a log note on its submission to *Atlantic* (Houghton Mifflin) on November 24 of that year. Chopin's notebook indicates a number of refusals before Way and Williams accepted the collection in 1898; but the firm was shortly transferred to Herbert S. Stone, and, for reasons that remain unclear, the manuscript was returned in February 1900.[2] By that time, the proposed contents had increased by at least six titles since she had submitted it to Houghton Mifflin four years earlier. Rankin's list of those contents probably dates from 1902 or 1903:[3]

"A Vocation and a Voice," "Elizabeth Stock's One Story," "Two Portraits," "An Idle Fellow," "A Mental Suggestion," "An Egyptian Cigarette," "The White Eagle," "Story of an Hour," "Two Summers and Two Souls," "Sketches," "The Unexpected," "Her Letters," "The Kiss," "Suzette," "Fedora," "The Recovery," "The Blind Man," "A Morning's Walk," "Lilacs," "Ti Démon," "The Godmother."

The general character of this proposed collection clarifies important shifts that were occurring in Chopin's fiction. First, only three (and a half, counting certain scenes in the title story) of the tales are set in Louisiana. Setting, the apparent inspiration of earlier fiction, was no longer a predominant, organizing feature. Indeed, the collection, which includes some of Chopin's most experimental stories, reveals how intently she had come to focus her fiction on human interiority, on the interplay of consciousness and circumstance, of unconscious motive and reflexive action. Such psychological elements, combined with technical control, indicate a writer not only in command of her craft but fully in tune with the intellectual currents of her time. In many ways, *A Vocation and a Voice* represents the culmination of Chopin's talents as a writer of the short story.

Since fully half of the stories in this new collection were written before the completion of *A Night in Acadie*, most are discussed with contemporaneous material in Chapter 4. The remaining eight, largely written between July 1896 and February 1899, are discussed here, and the two composed after the furor caused by *The Awakening* in the summer of 1899 are treated in Chapter 7.

The earliest (and only pre-1894) story Chopin intended for her third collection was the unpublished sketch "An Idle Fellow" (June 9, 1893). Anticipating "The Night Came Slowly" in its style and point, it begins as a weary meditation on studying in books and develops a reflective contrast with the refreshing sensuousness of nature. The piece implies a biographical mood, heightened by its portrait of a thrush longing for its mate—a familiar theme of Chopin's poetry—but its emphasis on the hidden life and on the juxtaposition of nature and God also marks its relevance to later works.

A subsequent, more polemical and dramatic sketch, "The Blind Man" (July 1896), might have been suggested by Maupassant's 1882 tale of the same name—"L'Aveugle." Both evoke the contrasting effects of the sun on the blind and the sighted and then dramatize the victimization of the sightless. Chopin's story makes a strong social comment, echoing other tales of that summer, including "Nég Créol" and "A Pair of Silk Stockings." But while resentment at oppression and indifference toward poverty suffuse the setting, Chopin's story is finally less pessimistic than Maupassant's, focusing on the ironies of fate as much as on human insensitivity. By presenting without explanation the horrified reactions of the crowd (to a person overrun by one of the "monster electric cars"), Chopin neatly delays the climax in order to imply a moral comment. Since our sympathies are identified with the blind man, we misread the crowd's alarm, which is actually for "one of the wealthiest, most useful and most influential men of the town." As we confusedly disengage ourselves from the crowd's perspective, the major irony surfaces: the moral blindness of those who are hostile or indifferent to the continuing tragedy of a poor blind man "stumbling on in the sun" while they are deeply touched by a wealthy man's violent end. Reiterating a familiar chord, Chopin affirms these moral ironies as intrinsic to a society whose morality is trapped in materialistic conventions.

Despite its quality, the title story, "A Vocation and a Voice" (November, 1896), was difficult to place. Loosely based on the life of William Marion Reedy, it finally appeared in his *Mirror* more than five years after it was written. Anticipating *The Awakening* in its frank assertion of the power of sexuality in human life, the tale understandably inspired the reluctance of editors. Like

Edna Pontellier, its unnamed male hero struggles to integrate life's sexual imperatives with his identity.

The boy is, also like Edna, an outsider. Though he lives with the Donnellys in their overcrowded household in "The Patch," a nineteenth-century Irish ghetto of St. Louis, he has a "vague sense of being unessential." When he is accidentally stranded and exposed for the first time to nature, in the guise of "Woodland Park" (St. Louis's Forest Park), the sense of being unessential frees him—as it did Huck Finn—from place and responsibility. He "lights out," as it were, in the company of two professional vagabonds, Suzima and Gutro.

Like the boy, they are also foreigners to the conventional culture, but their affinity with nature associates them with deeper mysteries. They are healers of body and spirit, and, though their methods are specious, they offer tangible consolations to sedentary and commonplace lives in the drab towns on their way. Even the boy learns a part; his gifted singing reveals to his grateful audiences his own "communion with something mysterious, greater than himself . . . something he called God." Nature's release of this instinctive religious spirit establishes the terms of conflict. The access to God provided by nature—including eros—is set against the dogmas and prohibitions of conventional religion. The tale thus schematically refines Chopin's critique of these human institutions.

The boy himself habitually relies on traditional religion. Under the French priest's influence in the 'Cadian village they visit, he gets a steady job, develops a "sense of honor," and reaffirms his loyalty to "the holy teachings of the church." But these attachments finally prove no match for the call of nature when the vagabonds are ready to leave the village:

> But the stars were beginning to shine and he thought of the still nights in the forest. A savage instinct stirred within him and

revolted against the will of this man who was seeking to detain him.

Just as he left the Patch, so he leaves the village, without regret. Nature and the freedom of the road are irresistible—and are rendered no less so by their embodiment in the voice of a woman.

For if the priest and the brotherhood the boy later joins represent the stability of traditional religious and social identity, Suzima incarnates the mystical forces of eros and spiritual freedom—much as the sea was later to do for Edna. Moreover, Suzima's natural sensuousness, which plunges the boy into adulthood, is framed and enhanced by nature at large. The autumn afternoon in the park initiates his awakening: the "wanton touches" of the wind and the "damp, aromatic" scents induce an Emersonian state of blessed "tranquillity and contemplation which seemed native to him." But the cultivated park merely prefaces the natural realities that the boy then enters, plunging headlong into self-revelation.

Suzima and Gutro, earth mother and "Beast," represent the alternative faces of that nature, first as healers of spirit and body, then as passion and its obverse, murderous possession. But it is nature itself that precipitates the boy's recognition. Like the townspeople along their route, he is deeply affected by the seductive arrival of spring, "the time when the realities of life clothe themselves in the garb of romance, when Nature's decoys are abroad; when the tempting bait is set and the golden-meshed net is cast for the unwary." The village priest's religious books and papers cannot quiet his new restlessness, and in this state he accidentally encounters Suzima at her bath. The effect is electric:

He saw her as one sees an object in a flash from a dark sky—sharply, vividly. Her image, against the background of tender green, ate into his brain and into his flesh with the fixedness and intensity of white-hot iron.

Starkly sensual and characteristically Chopin, the passage underlines the natural contexts—"the background of tender green"—of the boy's awakened passions, a context reiterated at their consummation, in the "magic splendor" of a shimmering, moonlit, spring countryside.

Sexuality now magnifies the tentative oneness with nature the boy had experienced in the park: "He seemed to have been brought in touch with the universe of men and all things that live." But this bewildering new existence (the antithesis of his initial alienation) also brings its obligatory shadow of death. The boy's blind impulse to kill Gutro shatters his springtime illusions of innocent passion, as he painfully comprehends "within himself a propensity toward evil, . . . a devil lurking unknown to him, in his blood, that would some day blind him, disable his will and direct his hands to deeds of violence." This self-recognition, as "some hideous being," terrifies him, and he deserts both the woman and nature's spontaneity for the familiar security of the monastery.

The brotherhood allows the boy to resist the "hideous, evil spectre of himself" and to assume instead a benevolent new identity as "Brother Ludovic." He feels reborn the day he enters this refuge and eventually believes that he has grown immune to the foolish dreams of freedom and sensuality provoked by the woman. The immense wall he proceeds to construct epitomizes his external barriers against internal dangers. But this Sisyphean task merely dramatizes his plight and that of his brothers, who adopt rigorous lives and hope by their separation from the world (or their rigid respectability) to silence the tumultuous and dangerous passions of being human. But to suppress all human passion in order to avoid its dark potential is, Chopin insists, illusion at best. Thus when Ludovic again hears the voice calling, it is "the cry of his own being that responded." Leaping from his wall back to nature, Ludovic overcomes the religious restraints that have hindered his reunion with

Suzima. He must follow the woman, who calls him to himself—to danger, perhaps, but to fulfillment as well.

Though "A Vocation and a Voice" suffers somewhat from the clarity of its oppositions, its themes and techniques make it an interesting gauge of Chopin's movement toward *The Awakening*. The tensions between religion and nature, spirit and flesh, freedom and constraint, had occupied her for some time and were the foundation of works like "Two Sketches," "A Sentimental Soul," and "Two Portraits." But the mediation of sexuality in achieving identity is also central here, as it is in "Athénaïse." "A Vocation and a Voice" draws together these themes and articulates Chopin's essentially positive view of eros as well as its opposition to the artifice of moral institutions. The story thus defines the forces that later deter Edna's efforts to integrate life's sexual imperatives with her identity and also affirms nature's catalytic role. Even Chopin's experiments here with refrains and repetition anticipate the novel and the increasing lyricism of her style.

The compulsions of passion are also the focus of the stories immediately preceding and following "A Vocation and a Voice." Two months earlier, for example, she had written "Ti Frère" (September 1896). Incomplete in its four surviving versions, this fragmentary tale depicts the self-destructiveness of passion, which Chopin treats as powerfully as she does its positive influences. Here passionate revenge illustrates one price of self-assertion: a costly denial of community and affection. Chopin's portrait of the seedy, isolated retreat where men like Bud Aiken gather to indulge in manly vices is wonderfully gothic and aptly dramatizes the dark perils of Ti Frère's proud, masculine self-sufficiency. This world sharply contrasts with the world of women, centered on Azémia's grandmother's porch, where sympathy and solicitude prevail and where the communal identity of Ti Frère ("little brother") is restored.

"A Mental Suggestion" (December 1896) adapts a more contemporary image for compulsion—hypnosis. Chopin's fascination with extrasensory perception is attested by both her fiction and her own experience. Her son Felix, for example, recalled a startling occurrence in the middle of a theater performance, when his mother suddenly declared that "something has happened to Lelia" and rushed home. Her intuitions were confirmed; the girl's dress had caught fire, though she had extinguished it.[4] In "A Mental Suggestion," conscious control of the physical world extends impressively to changing the color of a coat or spoiling coffee at a distance. But Chopin's point is exactly the limits of these powers when they are applied to emotions.

Graham is a stereotype of the scientist, kin to Hawthorne's Aylmer and other nineteenth-century rationalists, a would-be god interfering in others' lives and officiously taking notes. Though his psychic researches resemble schoolboys' pranks, he soon recognizes in them a dangerous power that "like some venomous, unknown reptile" stings him. Still, he risks his friends' love for the thrill of seeing himself "like some patriarch of old about to immolate a cherished object upon the altar of science—a victim to the insatiable God of the Inevitable." The irony is that not science, but passion—his own jealousy and his friend Faverham's love for Pauline—is the real "God of the Inevitable." For Chopin, that blind and blinding force, which links humanity to nature, is the "imperative impulse." Even the scientist acknowledges it and submits, Dante-like, to its supremacy:

> Graham looked up at the little winking stars and they looked down at him. He bowed in acknowledgement to the supremacy of the moving power which is love; which is life.

As usual, Chopin wrote little during the holiday season, but by February 1897, she had written one story and was turning out an important series of essays for *Criterion:* the consequence of an invitation, as she put it, "to exploit my opinions upon books and writers, and matters and things pertaining thereto" (CW, 709). These six columns over seven weeks represent Chopin's first formal critical work since her reviews for St. Louis *Life* in 1894; and the lively, gracious prose reveals her deepening convictions about art. An easy intimacy characterizes these essays, each introduced with a colloquial phrase or platitude ("I have a young friend . . ." "It has lately been my unhappy experience . . ."), their informality sustained by local allusions, witty exaggeration, and mildly self-deprecating humor—such as references to her faulty memory, "which retains only the most useless rubbish" (CW, 716). But these also support the illusion of spontaneous art on which Chopin so often insisted.

Neither the familiar tone nor her protestations that she has no opinions to offer, however, conceal Chopin's decided views on several matters, from the qualities of good fiction to the folly of censorship. But as in her stories, she "would not be guilty of advising anyone to do anything"—at least not directly; and she clothes her opinions in an urbane and pleasantly seductive nonchalance. The first piece, for example, of "As You Like It," pretends to be merely a charming anecdote about her conversations with a "young friend." But it is in fact a serious comment about art. Originality, brevity, and truth are cited as admirable, though these are just the qualities that "they" would suppress. In Chopin's relaxed repartee, she tellingly declares that "poetry and philosophy, and vagabondage, and everything delightful" are the necessary "illusions" that "men and the world, life and the institutions" are intent upon destroying. Couched in disarming anecdote, this insistence on the "delightful" truths that a pragmatic society declares mere illusion is, of course, the crux of many of her own disturbing fictions.

The second essay is less compact. Its opening anecdote meanders unevenly toward a review of a short-story collection, "Tales of Two Countries," by the Norwegian, Alexander Kielland. Chopin does comment revealingly on Kielland, however, remarking the simplicity and depth of his tales. And she also interposes a wry paragraph on her self-proclaimed dearth of opinions, as well as her dislike of "transplanted" ones, underscoring her own skillful withholding of judgment on characters.

But if Chopin often refrains from judgment in fiction, she is not so forbearing toward writers. Three other essays also address the work of contemporaries—Ruth McEnery Stuart, Joel Chandler Harris, and Thomas Hardy—and reflect the qualities she sought in her own work. The piece on Stuart, besides being the primary evidence of the two women's contact (or Chopin's personal acquaintance with any nationally known writer), engagingly combines anecdote with critical appreciation. Chopin's praise of Stuart's fiction centers on its "wholesome, human note," its fidelity to life, its fine dialect, and abundant humor. But her evocation of the snowstorm that marked their meeting also implies a metaphor for Stuart's elusive attractiveness. She is for Chopin a "delightful womanly woman" whose generous personality conceals "no unsheathed prejudices" to wound her fellow human beings. Evidently, Chopin was as impressed by this celebrity's unexpected warmth as by the beauty of the new snow, and her essay pays her an elegant tribute. Indeed, this warm admiration is confirmed in the poetic synopsis with which she inscribed Stuart's copy of *Bayou Folk*.[5]

Of Thomas Hardy's work, at least *Jude the Obscure*, Chopin was less flattering. She rebuked its lack of humor, its brutality and gloom, and especially its manipulation of character. For Chopin, an "impression of reality" was the touchstone of artistic quality and anything less was "immoral, chiefly because it is not true." But this uncomplimentary review is set within the larger "question of how much or how little knowledge of life should be withheld from the youthful mind." Chopin observes wisely that the notoriety of *Jude* (its removal from St. Louis libraries) had simply encouraged young people to seek it out, only to be disappointed by its lack of truth. Chopin could have little known that even "true" books, like her own, might be subject to the prudish, and ultimately foolish, attitudes she so faults here.

The next essay is only superficially a review of the memoirs of Mrs. Mackin (Sallie Britton), Chopin's friend from childhood. The piece transforms wonderfully into a reflection on Chopin's own incapacity to write memoirs – to "live through yesterday," as she once commented in her diary.[6] She creates a delightful dialogue between herself and a reminiscent friend recounting their mutual failure to reconstruct her history. The conversation reveals some interesting autobiographical snippets, but concludes with an ironically invented admonishment to "stick to inventions." Shifting then to editors, Chopin wittily quotes the contradictory opinions issued on the same story: one editor finding it trite, another delighted by it but judging its companion piece "no story at all." Like many another writer before and since, she finally despairs aloud of "the editor, the writer, and the public" ever being "at one."

Less unified than some others, the disparate comments of Chopin's last column constitute a major summary of her fictional creed. The first section, on magazines, underlines her experimental interests. She points enthusiastically to the "newer booklets, chiplets, [and] clap-traplets" where the modern holds sway. In contrast to the "old reliables" that never shock us, in these "we may find ourselves a little blown and dizzy from the unaccustomed pace, but, on the whole, invigorated" (CW, 718). Turning then to Joel Chandler Harris's *Sister Jane*, she praises individual chapters and characters, but sharply censures the novel's "weak, unjointed, melodramatic" plot. Harris, she concludes, should simply write truthful short stories about the people of middle Georgia: "We shall not demand a plot; just a record of their plain and simple lives is all we want." The remark is an eloquent statement of her own ambitions as well as the aspirations of much modern narrative. And her final comments on the current fascination with "mental energy and its compelling force" only confirm how deeply Chopin had intuited the tendencies of American fiction. Experimentation, fidelity to life, psychological probing —these were all values Chopin expressed in her fiction, including the collection she was currently constructing; her twentieth-century successors were to make them the measure of fine art.

Both stories that frame these essays deal with disappointed love. "Suzette" (February 1897) was placed more quickly than any of the previous year's work, appearing in the October *Vogue*. Finely crafted, it recalls "The Kiss" in its treatment of indifference and coquetry, despite a more conventional assessment of love. Each of the principal characters is a perpetrator or victim of indifference—or both—and the final striking image of Suzette's carnations, meant for flirtation, lying now "like a blood-stain upon her white neck" underlines the deadly consequences of such indifference, especially to love.

"The Locket" (March 1897) had a less fortunate fate. Though Chopin sent it to nine or ten editors over the next eighteen months, and considerably condensed the opening and transitional passages, it remained unpublished—perhaps accounting for its apparent omission from *A Vocation and a Voice*. That even revisions (several of which minimized its unusually late evocation of the Civil War) failed to sell the story must have also confirmed her convictions about the spontaneity of her art. In fact, neither major character is well developed, and the plot depends on a mistaken identity ploy that was better used in "The Story of an Hour." Nevertheless, the bivouac and the battle scenes—the only such in Chopin's fiction—are skillfully done, as are the seasonal and quotidian symmetries that broaden her comment on the folly of war. Finally, Octavie's confused grief in the midst of a glorious spring, like the birds' bewildered efforts to understand these desperate "children playing a game," epitomizes the tangled ironies of love and war, even as it anticipates the reversals that restore Octavie's lost lover and turn tragedy into comedy.

Chopin wrote two other stories before she began her third novel that June. "A Morning Walk" (April 1897) explores the twin themes of religion and nature that had occupied her for several years. Archibald, reminiscent of characters in "A Mental Suggestion" or "A Point at Issue!," is a man of science, curious about nature, but generally insensitive to its charms. Despite his obliviousness, on this particular spring morning he is intoxicated by the beauty of a young girl, Lucy (the light bearer), who becomes the sexual catalyst of his "second vision of spring." His impressions are explicitly sensuous: "her soft, curved lips made him think of peaches that he had bitten; of grapes that he had tasted; of a cup's rim from which he had sometimes sipped wine."

As for the boy in "A Vocation and a Voice," such sensuality is a direct prelude to religious experience. But despite Archibald's uncharacteristic entrance into church, Chopin carefully sidesteps any sentimentality toward religion itself. Archibald is not hypocritically reverential at the Easter service (a moment Chopin's fiction favors for enlightenment),[7] though the words of the sermon ("I am the Resurrection and the Life") do evoke a new "vision of life." Archibald sees not specific religious truths but "the poet's vision, of the life that is within and the life that is without, pulsing in unison, breathing the harmony of an undivided existence." The gospel, like nature, is finally a medium, not an end:

> [Archibald] listened to no further words of the minister. He entered into himself and he preached unto himself a sermon in his own heart, as he gazed from the window through which the song came and where the leafy shadows quivered.

As Chopin insists with other romantics like Emerson and Whitman, the sermons of the heart are the most instructive. The Easter vision of the former skeptic is by its context conventionally religious, but its content is interior and revolutionary—and central to Chopin's later fiction.

Chopin's next story, "An Egyptian Cigarette" (April 1897), is equally significant. Its vision, however, in Chopin's characteristic rhythm of oppositions, is one of despair. The plot is slight: a friend, "the Architect," offers the narrator an Egyptian cigarette that she smokes, inducing a dream of a woman's desertion in the desert and evident suicide. The narrator wakes and crushes the remaining cigarettes, unwilling to see what other visions, even raptures, their "mystic fumes" might induce.

What is startling about this story—apart from its account of an hallucinogenic experiment—is its evocative prose and its bleak, erotic despair, carefully controlled by the exotic dream setting. Though many of Chopin's earlier sketches share its features, the epiphanic structure, lyrical prose, and eastern atmosphere specifically relate this piece to the prose poem, an avant-garde form popularized by Baudelaire and Daudet and enjoying a modest American vogue at the close of the century.[8]

In Chopin's story, the symbolic atmosphere is heightened by the allegorical naming of the Architect—"something of a traveler," who ingratiates himself to fakirs and collects foreign curios. He quietly orchestrates the narrator's singular experience, requiring her withdrawal into a private meditative space and recalling Louise Mallard's earlier retreat into the self in "The Story of an Hour." Though the narrator's retirement is supposedly out of consideration for the women, who "detest the odor of cigarettes," she secretly congratulates herself "upon having escaped for a while the[ir] incessant chatter." Her singularity among females thus asserted, she then experiences a dream whose despair is uniquely, and by implication, universally, feminine.

Through the female consciousness that she enters, the smoker futilely pursues her lover into the desert. She has defied the conventional wisdom of the oracles who warned her that "the rapture of life" would be followed by desolation; she has worshiped her Bardja and believed that romance would last forever—the real dream of feminine life. But Bardja has grown tired of female "fetters, and kisses, and you." Love eventually bores the male, and he abandons his worshipper for the "great city where men swarm like bees . . . beyond, where the monster stones are rising heavenward in a monument for the unborn ages." Tired and indifferent, he looks upon her crouching in the sand and smiles sadistically, baring "his cruel white teeth." Later, her body broken and bruised by pursuit, the woman lies in the desert, "like a wounded serpent, twisting and writhing." The dream ends in a river, which refreshes at first and then overwhelms her. Finally, as for Edna, her fear dissolves into sensual images of the romantic raptures that have led so ineluctably to this mortal despair.

The smoker revives, deeply oppressed, having "tasted the depths of human despair." But it is an explicitly feminine despair, caused by the suffocating restraints of dependence, of godlike social conventions, of the oppressions of chatter and romance. And while the dream image of the "blue lily" (echoing the blue rose of Sand's Utopian island or Baudelaire's black lily of artistic perfection)[9] encourages the hope of other, better visions, the smoker can bear no more. Sharing this "weight of centuries" so vividly has darkened any happier possibilities, and she scatters the remaining cigarettes in the breeze. But she is, as she concludes, "a little the worse for a dream," for her disappointing adventure now threatens any further experiments, any further challenge to the conventional surfaces of the conscious life. Chopin's imagination of the possible costs of insight is both vivid and painfully realistic.

This version of female abandonment and despair clearly anticipates the emotional nucleus of *The Awakening*, which Chopin began writing just two months later. The symbolic dream of the defiant woman, who is forced to reckon with the costs of that defiance, is played out more realistically in the novel. But the core of frustration and abortive challenge survives intact. The lyrical prose of the dream vision, moreover, anticipates the subtle incantations of *The Awakening* with its rhythmic repetitions, its brief, sometimes broken, deceptively simple phrasing, and its symbolic details. With the composition of this strange tale, then, Chopin completed her technical novitiate and reasserted her primary themes. She was ready to begin her masterwork.

6

The Awakening

When Kate Chopin began her third novel in June 1897, her fictional powers were at their height. Her succinct, evocative style had been refined by the discipline of the short story and her recent experiments with the prose poem; she had mastered a wry and delicately distanced manner that artfully withheld moral judgments; and she had, with increasing confidence, focused on a theme of importance, the rift between consciousness and instinct, convention and conscience, each thoroughly complicated by sexual roles.

The heroine of *The Awakening* is twenty-eight-year-old Edna Pontellier, a Kentuckian married to a New Orleans businessman, Léonce Pontellier. Vacationing at Grande Isle, a genteel nineteenth-century resort on the Gulf Coast, Edna becomes romantically attached to Robert Lebrun, a young Creole bachelor. Though Robert abruptly departs for Mexico when he senses that his dalliance has become too serious, the sensuous atmosphere of the Gulf has already stirred vague longings in Edna that will not be again suppressed. Unsettled by the summer's events, she returns to her French Quarter home, where she soon ceases the social routine of visiting days, neglects the supervision of her servants, and increasingly abandons herself to moods and whims. Her incredulous husband, on a friendly doctor's advice, tries to placate her capriciousness, then leaves on a business trip without her when she refuses to accompany him. Still missing Robert and alone, her two young sons visiting in the country, Edna begins a half-hearted affair with the importunate rake Alcée Arobin. She makes plans to move away from Esplanade Avenue to a small "pigeon house" and gives a final birthday party to celebrate the event. Then Robert, whose affairs Edna has followed through their mutual friend, the ecccentric Mlle. Reisz, unexpectedly returns. Edna's pleasure is truncated, however, by his pusillanimous farewell note. He leaves the very evening he visits her, while she is attending her friend Adèle Ratignolle in childbirth. Depressed by the recognitions these events precipitate, Edna returns alone to Grande Isle. On the same beach where the summer before she had learned to swim, she mechanically casts off her clothes, and, reflecting on the people and events that have overcome her, Edna swims far out into the Gulf, to her death.

While few deny the economy and lyric power of this compelling tale, critics have differed widely in their assessment of Edna's struggle—a consequence, in part, of the novel's apparent lack of authorial comment. Several, for example, like Wolff or Ringe, stress the internal qualities of Edna's conflict and view her crisis as the futile efforts of an individual at integration.[1] Still others focus on the external forces inhibiting Edna, describing them variously as a "Victorian myth of love," "the rules of marriage," maternity, patriarchal roles, or "the social forces of Creole Louisiana near the end of the nineteenth century."[2] The meaning of Edna's suicide is likewise debated, with some, like Seyersted, pronouncing it "a triumphant assertion of her inner liberty" and others declaring it "a defeat and a regression, rooted in a self-annihilating instinct, in a romantic incapacity to accommodate herself to the limitations of reality."[3]

In fact, the central issue of Chopin's last novel is one she had addressed in her first: how does one (especially one female) achieve personal integrity in a world of conventional restraints? It is a problem Chopin constantly confronted as a writer; and the solutions at which she arrived implied both compromise and failure, embodying her vision in conventional motifs and styles, articulating it through familiar and acceptable materials. But while no writer manages to express her vision purely, without some accommodation of literary conventions and commercial expectations, by this point Chopin had developed, in the expressive fidelity of her style, a subtle vehicle for the complex realities she perceived. For her, uncompromising realism embodied her unique viewpoint: the tale itself reveals its truths. She had, to echo Elaine Showalter's fine distinction, learned to express the "wild zone" of her own perspective through the conventional restraints of a studied realism.[4] What she had yet to learn—as did Edna—was the outrage with which her simple effort at truth-telling would be greeted.

As in much of her fiction, Chopin's sense of a complex reality permits no easy answers to the moral questions raised by this conflict between the individual and social restraints. Instead, by withholding the moral of this moralistic tale and leaving the nature and value of Edna's awakening essentially unresolved, Chopin delineates the difficulty of calibrating the appropriate relationship between the self and society. The disconcerting ambiguity of the novel's resolutions thus only confounds our expectations of authorial judgment. Having engaged our sympathies by her vivid fiction, Chopin then forces us to appraise them by the harsh light of reality.

The crux around which Chopin fashions this study of the conflict between self and society is the uncertain figure of Edna Pontellier. Like Emma Bovary, the similarity of whose plight is often noted,[5] Edna is incurably romantic, unconsciously sensual, headstrong, indecisive, and an unlikely subject for the self-realization in which the novel engages her. Indeed, an early editorial chapter defines the nature and difficulty of her task with unmistakable wryness:

> In short, Mrs. Pontellier was beginning to realize her position in the universe as a human being, and to recognize her relations as an individual to the world within and about her. This may seem like a ponderous weight of wisdom to descend upon the soul of a young woman of twenty-eight—perhaps more wisdom than the Holy Ghost is usually pleased to vouchsafe to any woman.
>
> But the beginning of things, of a world especially, is necessarily vague, tangled, chaotic, and exceedingly disturbing. How few of us ever emerge from such beginning! How many souls perish in its tumult! (Ch. 6)

Chopin's characteristic irony here underlines both the folly and the urgency of Edna's need for self-understanding. Edna must willy-nilly come to terms with herself both as a distinct individual and in relation to a world "within and about her." Though Chopin understood clearly enough the universality of this imperative, she also recognized the peculiar difficulties faced by women. In her own era, women's roles were well defined—in relation to men—and presumably required no further differentiation. Encouraged to self-sacrifice rather than self-realization, women like Edna had to overcome tradition and biology as well as the intransigence of social structures in any effort at self-assertion. Even an essential reality like sexuality was too often disguised as romance, vaguely mingled with love.

But while these obstacles are formidable, and include Edna's personal weaknesses, Chopin faces squarely the consequences of Edna's recognition of "her position in the universe as a human being." Like her predecessor Adrienne in "Lilacs," Edna must bear the full brunt of both her freedom and her understanding, despite the unforeseen inadequacies limiting them. Fundamental to Edna's self-awakening is the recognition of her physical being, an awareness several of Chopin's female characters (and some males) also initially lack, but which constitutes a critical prelude to consciousness. Promoted by her motherless childhood and domineering father, Edna's customary reserve disguises a self-repression that she, like Louise Mallard, assumes is natural. But the sensual atmosphere of the Gulf, which permeates the novel, and the easygoing openness of Creole culture work to loosen this "mantle of reserve that had always enveloped her" (Ch. 7), leading Edna to a new awareness of her body and ultimately of the hidden self it expresses.

Though Edna's discovery of her own sensuality culminates in Arobin's embraces, it is implicit early in the novel. Attracted to Adèle, for example, by her "sensuous susceptibility to beauty," Edna responds readily to her friend's sympathetic caresses and unfolds to her with unaccustomed candor the recollections of the past that the "delicious picture" of the sea before them has inspired. Edna's initial childhood memory, which significantly reflects her spiritual condition, is primarily sensory: walking aimlessly through tall, green grasses in the hot summer sun. The unfamiliarity of Edna's physical awareness is also evident at Madame Antoine's where, having undressed for sleep, Edna is acutely conscious, as if "for the first time," of her own flesh. The sensual satisfaction she takes from her nap and from the meal that follows initiates a rhythm of sleeping and eating in the novel, underlining both the physical realities to which Edna is adjusting and the novel's central metaphor.[6] "Awakening" to her own physical being, Edna exults in her concrete individuality. Only later do the real consequences of that awakening become apparent.

As for Athénaïse, Edna's latent sensuality remains for a time veiled by the beguiling mists of romance. Confiding to Adèle, she recalls her repeated attachments to unattainable objects, from the "dignified and sad-eyed cavalry officer" who visited her older sister's friend in

Mississippi, to the "great tragedian" on whose portrait she projects her adolescent passions. Her engagement to Léonce was itself only recompense for the loss of the tragedian and an equally romantic defiance of her father. But, eventually recognizing "no trace of passion or excessive and fictitious warmth" in her affection for Léonce, Edna feels assured of a prosaic permanence in her marriage and calmly accustoms herself to this lesser reality. Robert, however, and the relaxed Gulf shores reawaken these dreams of a "great passion," propelling Edna upon a tentative, impulsive pursuit of her youthful desires.

Edna's recollection, for the first time since childhood, of her romantic dreams and the pleasures of the senses is profoundly related to her milieu. Chopin freely evokes the rich atmosphere of New Orleans and Grande Isle, drenching the novel with the "light and languour" (Ch. 2) of summer days and soft breezes, the seductive odors and sounds of the Gulf. Even when Edna returns to the city, it is "the soft, gusty beating of the hot south wind" (Ch. 19) and the images of Grande Isle that haunt her imagination and stir her emotions. This lush setting creates both a physical motive for Edna's behavioral changes and a resonant metaphor for the fervid sensuality those changes reflect.

Chopin couples this tropical sensuality with another theme familiar in her work: the outsider in Creole culture. A Protestant from the upper South, Edna is, like David Hosmer, "not thoroughly at home in the society of Creoles." Their "entire absence of prudery" is rather startling: she listens with shock and embarrassment to the risqué stories and detailed accounts of childbirth told in mixed company; she is astonished to find a racy novel openly discussed. That such freedom is accompanied by "a lofty chastity" is a paradoxical heritage of the Creoles' Catholic and European roots that Chopin had exploited in "Two Portraits." Secure in their Catholic convictions about the indissolubility of marriage and the adequacy of maternity for feminine fulfillment, the Creoles can afford the liberty of indecorous speech and a superficial physical intimacy. The unshakable reality of chastity is never threatened, and indeed, seems protected by these outlets. As an outsider – an American – whose Puritan legacy is a distrust of the body, Edna is unprepared for this lax environment that calls into question her own customary reserve. With its superficial freedoms, this alien culture, reinforced by the sensory stimulation of the Gulf, provides what has been called "a climate of psychological relaxation"[7] and the initial impulse for Edna's awakening.

But while these elements loosen Edna's repressions, they do not channel her energies in any specific way. Since the age of twelve when, she recalls, "religion took a firm hold upon" her, Edna has lived reflexively, "just driven along by habit." As these defining habits now slip away, she experiences a vague anguish, an unthinking aimlessness, to which she responds with impulse and caprice: refusing and then accepting Robert's invitation to the beach, later going out on her day for receiving guests, or moving to the pigeon house. As is often the case in Chopin (*cf.* Mrs. Sommers, Archibald, or Graham), such disorientation signals a critical transition, the chaos preceding insight.

The particular catalyst of Edna's reorientation is Robert. A romantic given to flirtatious poses with unavailable women, Robert embodies the unsatisfied passions of Edna's youth. His presence also focuses the sensuality disguised by her romantic dreams. Through Robert, Edna tentatively experiences the possibility of venturing beyond the prescribed patterns of her life. Not coincidentally, the sexual tension in their flirtation is revealed the very evening Edna learns to swim, a crucial image of her efforts at selfhood. Having failed all summer to master this art, Edna is one night like a "little tottering, stumbling, clutching child, who of a sudden realizes its powers, and walks for the first time alone, boldly and with over-confidence" (Ch. 10). Her new-found control immediately tempts Edna to excess, swimming "far out, where no woman had swum before." As Paula Treichler observes, the passage, with its implied warnings of premature confidence, pinpoints both the spiritual dimensions and sexual-political risks of Edna's act.[8] And anticipating her final swim as well as her experimental rejection of her former life, Edna's elation is immediately succeeded by a "quick vision of death," mirroring the inexperience and lack of strength that later undermine her efforts at selfhood.

Not unexpectedly perhaps, the independent spirit that the summer has evoked is first directed—tentatively and then deliberately—against the constraints of Edna's marriage. Rejecting, like Athénaïse, her housekeeping responsibilities and abandoning her visiting day (chiefly a public relations convenience for Léonce), Edna, on her return to the city, begins to assert her right to self-possession. Absorbed by his business ambitions and complacently patriarchal, Léonce is Chopin's most incisive portrait of the Americanized male. In his bourgeois insensitivity, he regards his wife's rebelliousness simply as illness or insanity. To him, she is essentially "a valuable piece of personal property," whom he expects to listen to his talk (Ch. 3), to make love when he is aroused (Ch. 11), to assist him socially in "keep[ing] up with the procession" (Ch. 17), to supervise his servants and his children, and generally, like the clerks in his office, to function efficiently and quietly toward his well-being and satisfaction.

For Edna, such activities have become empty and irrelevant, like ill-fitting clothes. Gradually, she discards the pretense, "casting aside that fictitious self which we assume like a garment with which to appear before the world" (Ch. 19). But if Edna's sensuality has led her to self-assertion, it also leads to Alcée Arobin. Deprived of Robert (who has withdrawn from the perils of their attraction to "business" in Mexico), Edna confusedly transfers the energy of her romantic affections to Arobin's seductive invitation. But her sexual responses to Arobin are always mingled with thoughts of Robert: Robert will be betrayed by her infidelity (Ch. 25), the happy news of his coming return weakens her resistance to Arobin (Ch. 27), and Robert's reproach—not Léonce's—haunts her when Arobin departs (Ch. 28). But Edna's first pleasurable sexual experience also abruptly clarifies a critical distinction between passion and love. At once she comprehends "the significance of life," the "beauty and brutality" of desire without affection, passion without the conventional drape of romance. Her "dull pang of regret" only anticipates the larger disappointment of the paradoxical realities to which she is awakening.

Edna's confusion of romance and passion—and the comprehension that the experience of passion brings—is familiar in Chopin's fiction. Convinced of the power of sensuality, Chopin recognized the consequences of its suppression, especially for women. Her concern is echoed in a letter she received after the novel appeared, a letter purportedly from Dr. Dunrobin Thomson, a British physician, but now suspected to have been from an anonymous friend. The writer observed that the frequent confusion of sex and romance by many nineteenth-century women was a consequence of their prudish sexual education. Taught "that passion is disgraceful," respectable women could only label their inevitable sexual urges as "love," and thus became unable to distinguish affection from mere physical attraction.[9] They remained emotional adolescents.

Edna's idealized fantasies of passionate union thus distinctly conflict with the experience she seeks as an individual. In her affair with Arobin, she recognizes the fallacy of her belief that sexuality and love—"her relations as an individual to the world within and about her"—are inseparable. Chopin delineates these irreconcilable desires (for selfhood and relationship) most notably in the characters of Edna's two closest friends, Mlle. Reisz and Adèle Ratignolle.

Held up as a model even by Léonce, Adèle perfectly embodies the social definitions of womanhood. Her marriage epitomizes the ideal "fusion of two human beings into one." Fulfilled by one another, the Ratignolles have submerged themselves in the roles society prescribes for intimacy: for women, that of wife and mother; for men, that of attentive provider. Possessing "every womanly grace and charm," Adèle represents exactly what Edna is not, a mother-woman, the dominant type at Grande Isle:

> It was easy to know them, fluttering about with extended, protecting wings when any harm, real or imaginary, threatened their precious brood. They were women who idolized their children, worshiped their husbands, and esteemed it a holy privilege to efface themselves as individuals and grow wings as ministering angels (Ch. 4).

But while Edna recognizes Adèle's "blind contentment" in this role, she sees in it "an appalling and hopeless ennui." Trying to explain herself to her friend, Edna says that she would readily give up the unessential (her money or her life) for her children, but she wouldn't, she insists, "give myself" (Ch. 16).

But if Edna cannot sacrifice "the essential" for her children, as Adèle evidently can, neither does she possess Mlle. Reisz's courageous soul. Independent and defiantly unmarried, Mademoiselle is also solitary, with "a disposition to trample on the rights of others." Edna admires the stiff courage of Mademoiselle's unconventionality, but she has neither her daring nor her willingness to live alone and celibate. Edna simply cannot reject the very sensual awareness that has promised her self-possession.

Edna's conflict is reiterated in three mysterious figures at the edges of the action on Grande Isle. The two lovers, like the Ratignolles, are complete as a pair, and totally anonymous in their love; the lady in black, meanwhile, whose constant devotions suggest nunlike habits, is always alone. Their shadowy presences signal Edna's dilemma; but by the time she has recognized the contradictions of their attractions, her life has severely limited her options.

If Edna's affair with Arobin gives her some control of her sexuality (an expression of individuality), her desire for a more complete relationship with Robert is thwarted. Her "soft, cool, delicate kiss" with its "voluptuous sting" unmistakably manifests her new-found initiative as well as her passionate intents. But Edna cannot fit Robert's reality to her dream of a mutually free, sensuous union.[10] Robert can see Edna only in conventional terms, and he is visibly shocked by her rebuke of his own "wild dream" that Léonce can free her from her obstructing marriage. "I am," she laughingly insists, "no longer one of Mr. Pontellier's possessions to dispose of or not. I give myself where I choose." Unable to conceive of a woman apart from the conventional garb of wife—or of passion without a saving respectability—Robert quietly leaves, too "honorable" to encumber their love with sex, too traditional to bear the consequences of Edna's new self-possession.

But if Robert's dream of propriety persists, Edna's dream of independence does not. The final limitations of her gender and history soon force themselves upon her in the narrative guise of Adèle's summons to her childbed. Edna and Robert's last *tête-à-tête* is thus tellingly interrupted by an unsubtle reminder of the consequences of the sexuality that Edna is inviting.

This apt intrusion dramatizes what for women, before effective and widely available birth control, was the principal obstacle to genuine sexual independence: childbearing. Edna's "vague dread" as she attends Adèle's sufferings gradually flares into a "flaming, outspoken revolt against the ways of Nature" (Ch. 37). Witnessing with "inward agony" the inescapable consequences of physical love, Edna at last perceives the real horns of her dilemma. While she can readily abandon the ill-fitting social garb of marriage to Léonce, she cannot ignore the children: neither her living sons, nor those—given the general inaccessibility of contraceptives—that would certainly result from her sexual activities. She can challenge the social obstacles to her new selfhood, but she is powerless against the "ways of Nature."

Edna's conversation with Dr. Mandelet probes this new and defeating awareness. As Mandelet gently explains, the illusions by which nature decoys people into procreation take no account of the "moral consequences, of arbitrary conditions which we create, and which we feel obliged to maintain at any cost" (Ch. 38). Edna's dilemma, like Hosmer's and Adrienne's and so many other of Chopin's characters, is that of finding one's self responsible for choices made in blindness. Edna's dreams of realizing herself in the union that romance promises have led her to sexual experience that, unlike the dreams, solidifies into reality. Having to awaken from those dreams is, to Edna, a bitter experience. Musing aloud, she wishes that "one might go on sleeping and dreaming—but to wake up and find—oh! well! perhaps it is better to wake up after all, even to suffer, rather than to remain a dupe to illusions all one's life" (Ch. 38). Edna's painful realities are those of Étienne and Raoul and of her biological destiny as female. But if Edna cannot return to her illusions, neither can she deny the "little new life" of her sensuous and self-determining nature. Unwilling "to trample up on the little lives," either of her children or of her self, Edna chooses to sacrifice the "unessential"—her mortal existence.

Lying awake after the pivotal discovery of Robert's farewell note, Edna despondently reconsiders all that has led her to this final choice. The next day, returning to the sea where her awakening had begun, she carries out her plan to elude the "soul's slavery" to which the children had threatened to reduce her. Stripping herself literally of the confining "pricking garments" she has been metaphorically discarding, Edna is at last herself "like some new-born creature, opening its eyes in a familiar world that it had never known," but a creature doomed by its unacceptable contradictions.

Deprived of the lover she had craved, Edna chooses his image in the sea: "sensuous, enfolding the body in its soft, close embrace" (Ch. 39). Throughout the novel, the sea is a powerful metaphor of her costly and ambivalent quest. Several critics have noted its symbolic and mythical overtones—its sensuality and connections with Venus, whom the naked Edna seems to conjure in the final tableau; its Freudian echoes of "'oceanic feeling,' the longing to recapture that [prenatal] sense of oneness and suffused sensuous pleasure" to which Edna seems subject; and its double promise of infinity and solitude.[11] Like the bluegrass meadow of her childhood, the sea elicits both fear and pleasure, a place with "no beginning and no end." Finally, Edna yields entirely to its seductions. From the beginning the promise of self-knowledge has beckoned: "The voice of the sea is seductive; never ceasing, whispering, clamoring, murmuring, inviting the soul to wander for a spell in abysses of solitude; to lose itself in mazes of inward contemplation" (Ch. 6). But the omission of the final clause in this refrain at the end of the novel, denoting a loss of temporality and the purposefulness of contemplation, indicates the abortive consequences of Edna's self-knowledge. Unable to reintegrate her new self into her constrictive society, she can only "wander in abysses of solitude" (Ch. 39). She has become indeed "A Solitary Soul," the title the novel bears in manuscript.

Opting for selfhood even though she knows she cannot sustain it, Edna imagines Mlle. Reisz's sneers for not having "the strong wings" that would carry her "above the level plain of tradition and prejudice" (Ch. 27). Her recollection here climaxes another significant image pattern, birds. So long caged by convention even in her illusory "pigeon house," Edna herself resembles the pet parrot and mockingbird that open the novel, speaking an incomprehensible language of selfhood and no longer able to fly. That association is echoed by the bird on the beach that she watches before her last swim. Alone and despondent, Edna see it, broken like herself, "reeling, fluttering, circling disabled down, down to the water" (Ch. 39). Evoking the improvident Greek youth, Icarus, Edna too has overestimated her power in the thrill of new-found freedom.

Other elements also underline Edna's visions of solitary selfhood. Mlle. Reisz's music, for example, to which Edna is particularly susceptible, conjures images of her ill-fated aspiration and deepens the links between the two women. One plaintive piece Edna calls "Solitude," for example, evokes the naked "figure of a man standing beside a desolate rock on the seashore" (Ch. 9) – a prophecy of her solitary fate. But although both women aspire to be artists, to create their own lives, only Mlle. Reisz possesses the courage to defy traditions. Even as Edna cannot fulfill her promise as a painter, so can she not realize her visions of selfhood.

Mademoiselle's music also suggests the emotional roots and lack of conscious control in Edna's quest. Spawned in the sensual release of the Creole life at Grande Isle, Edna's consciousness is stirred to life by Mademoiselle's playing on the same moonlit night that she both learns to swim and recognizes her desires for Robert. The music, Chopin tells us, arouses not the images Edna had experienced before but the "very passions themselves" within her soul, "swaying it, lashing it, as the waves daily beat upon her splendid body" (Ch. 9).

Like the ocean, Mademoiselle's music speaks to Edna's deepest self. And it is the invitation of that self—neither fully conscious nor rational—that Edna pursues, leading her to follow blindly "whatever impulse moved her, as if she had placed herself in alien hands for direction, and freed her soul of responsibility" (Ch. 12).

Edna's path to integrity then is not a way deliberately chosen. Her ineffectual efforts and ultimate failure to think through her situation reiterate the irrational, emotional forces that have impelled her toward her destiny. With her iconoclasm more fate than will, Edna epitomizes the ambivalences that Chopin's fiction had unflinchingly confronted throughout its course. Edna's desire for integrity, like the familiar patterns and happy endings of local color, has undeniable appeal. But just as life often contradicts those hopeful patterns, so does an intransigent social and physical reality thwart Edna's efforts at selfhood. And having seen the attraction and value of one and the force and obstinacy of the other, Chopin could deny neither. But if Edna's fate implies a pessimistic appraisal of the individual's chances against the world, Chopin also insists on Edna's triumph. Like Mrs. Mallard or Mrs. Summers or Athénaïse, Edna at least knows the possibilities for selfhood, even if reality painfully denies them.

Like any ambitious writer, Kate Chopin must have eagerly awaited the reviews of *The Awakening* after its publication on April 22, 1899. As her most unflinching portrayal of womanhood to date, she surely had high hopes for it. Her anticipation was doubtless proportionate to the disappointment she must have felt when the St. Louis *Mirror* published the first notice twelve days later. Setting a pattern from which there were to be few deviations, Frances Porcher's essay praised the art of the novel as unblemished, but then panned its subject as depressing and altogether dismaying, wondering aloud if the story was too unseemly to be worth the telling at all. Singled out for particular criticism was the nature of Edna's awakening: "One would fain beg the gods," Porcher wrote, "in pure cowardice for sleep unending rather than know what an ugly, cruel loathsome monster Passion can be when, like a tiger, it slowly stretches its graceful length and yawns and finally awakens."[12] The other St. Louis papers quickly followed suit. The *Daily Globe Democrat* said that the book was "morbid" and "not healthy"; the *Post-Dispatch* called it "too strong drink for moral babes, [that] should be labelled 'poison.'"[13] Her friend C. L. Deyo was kinder, praising Chopin's "complete mastery" of her art and commenting that the novel displayed her best qualities – a "delicacy of touch of rare skill in construction, the subtle understanding of motive, the searching vision into the recesses of the heart." But Deyo then went on to condemn what seems to have bothered many early critics – the revelation that a woman's passion might be more powerful than her sense of duty or remorse: "A fact, no matter how essential, which we have all agreed shall not be acknowledged is as good as no fact at all," he intoned, "and it is disturbing – even indelicate – to mention it as something which, perhaps, does play an important part in the life behind the mask."[14] From New Orleans to Los Angeles, critics expressed dismay that Chopin not only acknowledged the unseemly fact of feminine sexuality, but also never sounded "a single note of censure of [Edna's] totally unjustifiable conduct."[15] In other words, Chopin not only portrayed an indelicate subject; she also failed to make her heroine a moral exemplar of what women got when they deserted "good" husbands and abandoned innocent children. Several reviewers (including Willa Cather) went so far as to recommend that Chopin return to a "better cause," to subjects and themes "more healthful and sweeter of smell."[16]

The overwhelmingly unfavorable response to Chopin's most earnest attempt at realism evidently caught her by surprise. She had written the book in a mood of confidence. She had felt that her sharpening vision of womanhood was being appreciated and that the truths she was telling had struck responsive chords. But the reproving reviews continued to amass. Disheartened and taken aback by the furor, she was eventually persuaded by her friends to defend herself publicly. However, her brief rejoinder in *Book News,* dated May 28, is fraught with wry humor and expresses no more real remorse than Edna herself had displayed:

> Having a group of people at my disposal, I thought it might be entertaining (to myself) to throw them together and see what would happen. I never dreamed of Mrs. Pontellier making such a mess of things and working out her own damnation as she did. If I had had the slightest intimation of such a thing I would have excluded her from the company. But when I found out what she was up to, the play was half over and it was then too late.[17]

Indeed, even Chopin's retraction acknowledges the stubborn realities that her novel was trying to express. Like most Victorian women, even Edna had recognized only "too late" what she was up to; but exposing the consequences of her too-common dilemma was exactly what Chopin had been up to.

As Virginia Woolf once remarked, it is the nature of writers to care very deeply about adverse criticism. Having, as her friend John Dillon suggested, "poured herself—thoughts and feelings—into the novel with utmost honesty,"[18] Chopin felt herself and her work completely rejected. Most painfully, she felt that her chances for literary success had been obscured by the scandal, and that fear must have contributed greatly to the creative paralysis she began to experience. The remaining years of her life saw but a trickle of stories where the former stream had been.

But while Chopin's own discouragement was intense, her novel proved more resilient. The recognition of its revolutionary achievement took some sixty years, but the power of *The Awakening* is once more apparent. Even now, withholding its own judgments, the novel quietly implicates us in its probing of such moral questions as the nature of sexuality, selfhood, and freedom, the meaning of adultery and suicide, and the relationship between biological destiny and personal choice. It is a novel that moves and disturbs us by its confrontation with the sheer obstinacy of our collective and individual humanity. And the subtlety of that confrontation assures *The Awakening* a permanent place in the American literary canon.

7

Poems and Final Stories: Epilogues

Chopin's preoccupation with writing *The Awakening* temporarily interrupted her normal, steady appearances in the magazines. Her last publication had been the April 1897 story "Suzette," which ran in the October *Vogue*. With the exception of a single translation in a St. Louis paper, it was her last publication before her novel was released two years later.[1]

Though Chopin did complete three or four short stories in the months following *The Awakening*, she soon redirected her creative energies to poetry. Her first publication had been a poem, but her efforts in this genre were episodic and are unreliably dated.[2] Several poems, for example, appear to have been written around 1893, when, in June, she collected six to send to *Vogue*. All but one were returned. Her stories, however, were selling very well that summer, and she seems to have laid her poetic ambitions aside, just as, with the failure of *Young Dr. Gosse*, she soon turned away from the novel as well. It was two years before any other poems appeared—three in mid-1895 and then a spate of occasional poems that Christmas to accompany gifts. Only in 1898 is there more verse, but its quantity—nearly twenty poems between May 1898 and February 1899—is significant. Perhaps the acceptance early that summer of her first novel in seven years encouraged her to reattempt poetry as well; or perhaps there just weren't any stories "writing themselves" as she had once insisted they must.[3] In any event, her notebooks indicate that the submissions of these verses in 1899 bore little fruit, and by that spring, stories again displaced them. Though Chopin took herself seriously as a poet, only three of her poems were ever published; three others were set to music and printed in the Wednesday Club program in 1899. One of these appeared as a popular song in 1913.[4]

Even in the context of most contemporary "magazine poetry," Chopin's verse is not particularly distinguished. Her subjects tend to the conventional; her imagery and technical control are not remarkable; her diction is often artificial. Still, both the quantity of her verse—nearly fifty poems—and its occasional quality are notable, especially insofar as these pieces sharpen our insight into her mind and art.

For the sake of discussion, we can observe four major groupings of Chopin's poetry: love poetry, nature poems, philosophical pieces, and occasional verse. Love poetry dominates her early efforts. Typically, as in "Psyche's Lament" (1890?) or "Good Night" (1894?), Chopin plays on the sensuous associations of darkness and love-longing to express the pain of separation. Such melancholy, with its autobiographical cast, also informs "If It Might Be" (1888), a simple pair of iambic quatrains expressing the speaker's devotion to her lover—to die or to live as he requires. The paradoxes of sweet death and ambivalent life create here the faint but characteristic irony by which Chopin usually controls the latent sentimentality of her themes. Such irony is more evident in poems with a stronger sensuality. "If Some Day" (August 16, 1895), for example, which Chopin sent hopefully to the *Chap-Book* in 1896,[5] dramatizes the same secret, erotic currents that she explores in "A Respectable Woman" or "Her Letters." Similar effects are apparent in "If the Woods Could Talk" (1893) and "By the Meadow Gate" (October 24, 1898), both of which use an archaic pastoralism to distance erotic motifs.

Chopin's celebrations of nature, particularly spring, form another related group of poems. While the earliest of these, "The Song Everlasting" (1893?), is unreservedly jubilant, later versions of the theme involve more irony and ambivalence. For example, "In Spring" (1898?), Chopin's last published poem, subdues its joyous initial note to a sobering temporality, while another poem of that summer pointedly warns against disobeying Robert Herrick's famous injunction to "Gather ye Rosebuds while ye may": "I'll gather the roses"—tomorrow—results in "scattered crumbs . . . all dry and dead." The disappointment of postponed opportunities in "The Roses" (July 11, 1898) must have given force to "The Storm," written a few days later, in which the lovers are decidedly more thrifty.

Such temporal paradoxes seem particularly pressing in Chopin's later poems. Noteworthy for its lack of rhyme, "One Day" (1899?), for example, gracefully evokes the sensual joys of "one most perfect summer day." The poem's combination of intense pleasure and calm acquiescence to the day's finitude subtly varies the *carpe diem* theme—and marks a very characteristic mood in Chopin's verse, one that is also apparent in her several rather apt imitations of Omar's *Rubaiyat*.

A few late poems also hint at art as a solution to time's inevitable progress. The trees of "White Oaks" (August 24, 1898), for example, are transformed in the poem from reminders of mortality to an emblem of eternity, like Wordsworth's "Daffodils," illuminating a moment out of time. The delicate word play of "With a Violet-Wood Paper Knife" (1899) suggests a similar transformation. Unlike the fading harbinger of spring, one may seek "the violet hid in the wood" at any season, its perfume captured, like Keats's maiden, forever. But the most curious version of this theme is "Ah! Magic Bird" (1899?). The song of the bird fades with the seasons, but nature's "flaming poppies" offer the "song of birds that never take their flight." While these pentameter quatrains are not technically remarkable, their allusion to hallucinatory experience interestingly parallels "An Egyptian Cigarette."

Much of Chopin's nature poetry, with its fascination with temporal paradoxes, is closely linked with her philosophical verse. This latter group is distinguished primarily by its directness. One of the most straightforward is "Because— ":

Because they must, the birds sing.
The earth turns new in Spring
Because it must—'Tis only man
That does because he can
And knowing good from ill,
Chooses because he will—

The thought is simple but well expressed, and Seyersted cites the piece as evidence of Chopin's rejection of the socioeconomic and biological determinism of her time—at least for human beings.[6] Similarly, a couplet from the same period seems to affirm her continuing theism, despite her lapsed Catholicism:

I wanted God. In heaven and earth I sought,
And lo! I found him in my inmost thought.

This interiority of the divine is reiterated throughout Chopin's fiction, too, of course, as in "The Night Came Slowly" or "A Morning Walk." Two quatrains written soon after the unfavorable reviews of *The Awakening* reflect a similar personal stoicism. Both "Life" (May 10, 1899) and "A Little Day" (1899?) express the poignant mingling of "dreams and a touch of pain" that define human life and also perhaps articulate Chopin's dismay at the rejection of one of her most deeply felt fictions.

The most interesting of this philosophical group, however, is "An Ecstasy of Madness" (July 10, 1898). With its run-on quatrains and feminine rhymes, its colloquial phrasing and exotic imagery, the poem readily suggests the work of Emily Dickinson, which had appeared in 1890:

> There's an ecstasy of madness
> Where the March Hares dwell;
> A delirium of gladness
> Too wild to tell.

The spring delirium, however, soon dwindles into a faint cynicism, so that what in an early verse is merely a picturesque reminder of an empty firmament—"a blinking star"—becomes by the final stanza a dull and passive indicator of loss. Left "here a-praying/To a blinking star," humanity must suffer the careless irresponsibility of those reckless heavenly bodies now "gone a-Maying." Futility and desperation, an undercurrent in much of Chopin's later fiction, mark this newly ambivalent "ecstasy of madness."

Most of Chopin's remaining poems are brief occasional pieces. Although one or two are noteworthy for their wordplay ["To Hilder Schuyler" (Christmas 1895) or "To Billy" (Christmas 1895)], a Jonsonian gratitude for hospitality ["To Henry One Evening Last Summer" (October 21, 1898)], or a charming evocation of long friendship ["To the Friend of My Youth: To Kitty" (1900?)], generally these have minimal poetic merit.

One final, apparently occasional, poem, however, deserves attention for its implied relationship to *The Awakening*. Written just as Chopin might have been reading proof, "The Haunted Chamber" (February 1899) articulates the powerful ambivalence a writer experiences for her creations. In conversational tones, the poem recapitulates an evening's *tête-à-tête* discussing "a fair frail passionate woman who fell." The convivial atmosphere makes the tale "more of a joke/Than a matter of sin or a matter of shame," and neither conversant finds anyone at fault. This suspension of judgment, however, is less possible when her friend has gone and a woman's faint wail fills the speaker's room. Her response to the woman's tremulous anguish is nevertheless flippant and ironic; not only is the woman dead, but her protest is dismissed in a cliché: "women forever will whine and cry." However, the lament's persistence contradicts the speaker's determined distance from "the torment with which I had nothing to do." And the final repetition of the cliché incorporates a resigned acknowledgment that such pain cannot be easily ignored. At the very least, "men must forever listen – and sigh." Though its couplets are unsophisticated, the poem is a remarkable statement of authorial ambivalence. As an artist indifferent to her heroine's fall, Chopin cannot yet wholly ignore the passionate pain her art has contained. And even her flip clichés betray the necessity of emotional response to her creation, as well as her concealed hope for its immortality.

Chopin's renewed concentration on poetry after *The Awakening* did not entirely interrupt her fiction. Indeed, the handful of stories she wrote as she awaited the release of her novel manifest her polished skill in story-telling as well as her continuing experimentation. Among them, "The Storm" is one of her most remarkable tales, while at least two others, "Elizabeth Stock's One Story" and "The Godmother," she considered good enough to add to her proposed list for *A Vocation and a Voice.*

Her first story after completing her novel, "A Family Affair" (December [?], 1897), was quickly syndicated by the American Press Association. Its lively heroine and subtle moral probing typify Chopin's next several fictions. Central here is a power struggle between the young, self-confident Miss Bosey and her avaricious and manipulative aunt, Félicie Solisainte, whose housekeeper she becomes. A deft use of gesture and props dramatizes this strife, from Bosey's bustling arrival and her first surprise for her mountainous aunt—moving her from her backyard watchpost to the "sweet, peaceful view" of the front room—to her confiscation of the keys and the replacement of both Dimple's pinned-up dress and the cook. Turning her aunt's own audacity and deceit against her, Bosey blithely transforms Félicie's paranoid existence into that of a sociable, refined dowager, cheerfully restoring the silver and linen and jewelry that Félicie had stolen from Bosey's mother and securing herself a husband in the bargain. This indirection is echoed narratively by centering awareness on the immobile Félicie, who must learn of Bosey's revolutionary activities through her spy, Dimple. Félicie is, as Bosey promised, returned to her feet, but by rage, not health—and then too late. Her restoration of her household to its crimped ways, like her restored mobility, only underlines the comic irony of her undoing: her effort to steal her niece's labor as housekeeper, like her use of everyone she meets, backfires spectacularly.

Such sprightly humor also informs Chopin's next tale, "A Horse Story" (March 1898). Chopin's only animal story, it is rather thin and sentimental—about going home to die and recognizing one's true love. But the irreverence of this hardheaded, self-possessed Indian pony, who condescends to understand French and broken English but who thinks and curses in his native Indian tongue, is nonetheless delightful.[7]

Chopin's next story also focuses on betrayal, but with a darker, subtler humor. Unusual in its use of first-person narration and a frame, "Elizabeth Stock's One Story" (March 1898) is fascinatingly self-reflexive, embodying Chopin's latest meditations on the difficulties of writing. The tale opens tersely:

Elizabeth Stock, an unmarried woman of thirty-eight, died of consumption during the past winter at the St. Louis City Hospital. There were no unusually pathetic features attending her

> death. The physicians say she showed hope of rallying till placed in the incurable ward, when all courage seemed to leave her, and she relapsed into a silence that remained unbroken till the end.

This bare, reportorial recitation countermands any sentimental response to Elizabeth's death, just as the narrator's later discovery of Elizabeth's lone manuscript belies the "unbroken" silence of her tragic end.

In direct contrast to the frame's impersonal tone, Elizabeth Stock's voice is colloquial and elliptical, explaining her frustrated ambitions with an easy intimacy:

> Since I was a girl I always felt as if I would like to write stories. I never had that ambition to shine or make a name; first place because I knew what time and labor it meant to acquire a literary style. Second place, because whenever I wanted to write a story I never could think of a plot. Once I wrote about old Si' Shepard that got lost in the woods and never came back, and when I showed it to Uncle William he said: "Why, Elizabeth, I reckon you better stick to your dress making: this here ain't no story; everybody knows old Si' Shepard."
>
> No, the trouble was with plots.

Elizabeth's humorous difficulty with plots markedly echoes Chopin's 1896 essay "In the Confidence of a Story-Writer," which describes her struggles with historical romance. Both authors reach the same conclusion: "It was no use." Good fiction, Chopin insists, must spring from experience; imitation or contrivance only betrays a writer into silence. The one story Elizabeth Stock finally tells thus has no conventional plot. She simply has a pen in her hand, some peace and quiet, and a soft autumn breeze that makes her feel like telling "how I lost my position, mostly through my own negligence, I'll admit that."

Elizabeth loses her position as postmistress, not because of negligence, as she believes, but because of her conscientiousness and its crass beneficiary's lack of scruples. Accidentally reading a postcard summoning Stonelift's richest resident, Nathan Brightman, to an urgent business meeting, Elizabeth ventures out into a storm to deliver it and catches a consumptive cold. Sometime later, she is removed for reading postal cards. Though she fails to make the appropriate connections, Brightman has coldly—and ironically—sacrificed her in the name of distorted priorities.

Though its social satire links this bitter little tale with "Miss McEnders" and "The Blind Man," its chief significance lies in its creation of Elizabeth Stock. Naive and unsophisticated as any country "stock," she is one of Chopin's strongest, most self-possessed females: "My name is Elizabeth Stock. I'm thirty-eight years old and unmarried, and not afraid or ashamed to say it." No woeful "old maid," she has been a proud, independent woman of responsibility who, after twenty years, has even trained her would-be suitor, Vance Wallace, not to wait on her. Though frustrated in her efforts to write popular fiction, Elizabeth has risen well above any conventional characters she might invent. And, appropriately, her writing—her style—defines her most vividly. The same elements that create humor, for example (her informality and clichés, her digressions, her deference to Uncle William's reported opinions, and her impatience with Vance), also establish her frank intimacy, her powers of observation, and the quality of her independence. Similarly, her casual inclusion of significant sensory details and homely but accurate similes indicates a person sensitive to the physical universe if not to social interactions.

Finally, Chopin's naive narrator conveys a complex transparency, revealing depths and subtleties to which she herself is oblivious. Simultaneously, her persona reflects both the naive emptiness of much popular fiction and the overlooked drama of much real life. Indeed, the final irony of Elizabeth's tale, without any aspiration to plot or sensation, is its revelation of a world as treacherous and evil and suspenseful as that of any dime novel. Confirming Chopin's notions of realistic fiction, this one story conceals a high degree of technical contrivance and sophistication in its artlessness. Chopin's continuing experimentation with authorial technique is obvious, as is the confident artistry manifested by the story's unstereotyped heroine, its moral probing, and its distillation of local color into style and voice. And though several editors refused it, Chopin evidently meant "Elizabeth Stock's One Story" to stand at the head of *A Vocation and a Voice*, immediately after the title story.

During the rest of the spring, Chopin wrote a few poems and completed her last translation of Maupassant, "Father Amable" (April 21, 1898). As Seyersted remarks, it was a confident period: Way and Williams had accepted not only her novel but *A Vocation and a Voice* (which was later returned); she had published three books and completed two rather more daring ones; "she must have felt that she could do almost anything."[8] What she did, that summer, was write a brief "Sequel to 'The 'Cadian Ball'" called "The Storm" (July 19, 1898). The story, which picks up five years after the matches made between Calixta and Bobinôt, Alcée and Clarisse, concerns Calixta's and Alcée's adulterous encounter during a sudden summer storm. Remarkable on several counts, the story is most startling in its approach to sexuality. As several critics have observed,[9] not even Chopin's European contemporaries, much less her American ones, dared to describe sexual intercourse at once so positively and so sensuously:

> They did not heed the crashing torrents, and the roar of the elements made her laugh as she lay in his arms. She was a revelation in that dim, mysterious chamber; as white as the couch she lay upon. Her firm, elastic flesh that was knowing for the first time its birthright, was like a creamy lily that the

sun invites to contribute its breath and perfume to the undying life of the world.

The generous abundance of her passion, without guile or trickery, was like a white flame which penetrated and found response in depths of his own sensuous nature that had never yet been reached.

When he touched her breasts they gave themselves up in quivering ecstasy, inviting his lips. Her mouth was a fountain of delight. And when he possessed her, they seemed to swoon together at the very borderland of life's mystery.

He stayed cushioned upon her, breathless, dazed, enervated, with his heart beating like a hammer upon her.

Much of the impact of this passage—despite occasionally stilted diction—derives from its imagery. Religion and nature, the two realms that Chopin consistently associated with human sexuality, mingle here. The religious imagery is hinted at earlier in the story, after Alcée is driven in from the gallery to the sitting room. The increasing sexual tension is introduced by his glimpse of the adjacent bedroom, "dim and mysterious" with its "white, monumental bed," intimating an inner sanctum, a holy place. And later, as Calixta's and Alcée's desires intensify, the Song of Songs is evoked, while the lovers' discovery of new dimensions of sensuous self-knowledge is rendered precisely in terms of hidden, sacred truths.

But if the sexual act is holy, it is also natural. Through it, Calixta obtains her flesh's birthright, while the lovers' congruence with the storm expresses the naturalness of their act and the story's central metaphor—the unleashing of fierce passion and sudden adultery. Chopin introduces the storm from a distance, showing its effect first on little Bibi and his father, Bobinôt. For them, the extraordinary stillness, the "sombre clouds that were rolling with sinister intention from the west" and the "sullen, threatening roar," initially have only literal implications. These deepen, however, as the tale turns to Calixta, who is as surprised by the storm as she is by Alcée's and her own passions; the preliminary obstacles to them, however—the husband and child described at Friedheimer's store—are soon overcome by the rain. Chopin adroitly matches the storm's irresistible development with the effects of passion on the two former lovers—from the lightning bolt that occasions their first physical contact, to the convenient veil of the heavy rain as they lie in bed, to their ultimate consonance with the storm's climax and gentle, exhausted retreat. By the storm's end, both the literal, two-year drought and the metaphorical one of the lovers' estrangement have ended. Just as the storm has released its pent-up energies, so have Alcée and Calixta vented the repressed sexuality of their physically unsatisfying marriages.

The consequences of this storm, however, underline yet another revolutionary aspect of the story, its moral indifference. Calixta's and Alcée's encounter ends complacently:

> The rain was over; and the sun was turning the glistening green world into a palace of gems. Calixta, on the gallery, watched Alcée ride away. He turned and smiled at her with a beaming face; and she lifted her pretty chin in the air and laughed aloud.

For Bobinôt and Bibi, to whom the storm was an immediate threat, its passing brings an unexpected freedom, and Calixta's compensatory concern for their comfort on their return, together with her renewed, animated spirits, enlivens her family, so that they all "laughed much and so loud that anyone might have heard them as far away as Laballière's."

For Alcée, as for his partner, the storm releases a rain of solicitude for his distant wife and children. His affectionate letter is richly ironic: he is indeed "getting on nicely," and his eagerness for Clarisse to stay longer implies the possibility of further rendezvous with Calixta. The storm's fortuitous eruption has not only renewed "all the old-time infatuation and desire for her flesh" but has freed Alcée from his narrow conceptions of honor. As long as she was inviolate, his honor restrained him. But her marriage and the chance storm make her "in a manner free to be tasted." Thus Alcée, whose honor had also prohibited marrying beneath himself, finds in the storm honor's appeasement and the means to satisfy his lust without compromising his definition of integrity.

Then, in the fifth section, like the last faint echo of the storm, we glimpse Clarisse in far-off Biloxi. Marriage, it appears, has been especially confining and burdensome to her, the lady among the four. On the coast, away from a husband whose passionate attentions she evidently does not relish, she has experienced "the first free breath since her marriage," and—like Athénaïse—the restoration of the "pleasant liberty of her maiden days." For her, the storm, though distant, has also been refreshing, giving her a welcome respite from conjugal obligations.

"So the storm passed and every one was happy." Since Chopin never attempted to publish this story, we may surmise that she well recognized the revolutionary implications of that final sentence. The reception of *The Awakening*, still to come, indicates that she had already overestimated the public's tolerance for a nonjudgmental attitude toward adulterous mothers. There is, to be sure, much room for irony in that final statement. Indeed, "The Storm" is not only a sequel to "At the 'Cadian Ball," with its manipulative and class-conscious pairings, but a comment on *The Awakening* as well. Edna's repressed sensuousness finds occasion just as Calixta's does; sexual expression is as natural and inevitable a birthright as individual autonomy. Only circumstance makes Calixta's and Alcée's affair comic while Edna's is ultimately tragic.

Chopin's next story, "The Godmother" (January

1899), also explores sudden passion. But violence, not desire, is the force in question here, and judgment is not escaped. This long tale is, in fact, a Dostoevskian murder mystery: the cover for homicide is perfect, but guilt, "the unwritten law" (Chopin's alternate title), proves more exacting than any human justice. Central to its careful plotting is Tante Elodie, a beloved and sprightly woman of sixty who, like Elizabeth Stock, has no regrets for her single state. The only remnant of her one brief passion for Justin Lucaze, thirty-five years before, is an unconnected, but "deep and powerful affection" for Justin's son, Gabriel. Ironically, it is precisely this love that destroys them both. When Gabriel accidentally murders a man, Elodie instantly shields him, persuading him to conceal his deed. But Gabriel's remorse is only compounded by her loving complicity, and, furthermore, her actions prevent his expiation, destroying in him "the last spark of human affection." When his physical frenzy has finally accomplished his death wish, Elodie, too, suffers the death of feeling. The poisoning effect of her well-intentioned gesture underlines the inevitability of evil. Her final recollection of her distant, broken-down plantation—"all dismantled, with bats beating about the eaves and negroes living under the falling roof"—mirrors her inner life, dismantled and desolate. Like Graham in "A Mental Suggestion," Elodie must confront alone the silent stars that witnessed her complicity and from whose judgment no one can hide.

"A Little Country Girl" (February 1899) was Chopin's last work before the reception of *The Awakening*. About a child forbidden and then permitted to go to the circus, the tale's chief interest lies in its fine evocation of childish frustrations and anticipations. Chopin sent the piece to *Youth's Companion* the very day she finished it; and though her notebook indicates that she was paid fifty dollars, the manuscript apparently remained unpublished. It was three years before a Chopin story again graced the pages of the *Companion.*

While this decision not to publish the story may or may not reflect the editors' sensitivity to Chopin's new infamy, the next pieces that she wrote certainly echo hers. In November, at the urging of her friends, Chopin wrote an essay for the *Post-Dispatch.* The glowing introduction and full-page headline—"A St. Louis Woman Who Has Won Fame in Literature"—may well be the work of her friend, editor C. L. Deyo. "As a writer of fiction," it says,

> Mrs. Chopin appeals to the finer taste, sacrificing all else, even pecuniary profit, to her artistic conscience. Her style is clear, frank and terse, never a word too many or too few. . . . Her art is not a cunning composition, but a living thing . . . she is an artist, who is not bound by the idiosyncrasies of place, race, or creed.[10]

Like her earlier columns for *Criterion,* this one begins anecdotally and quickly establishes the breezy intimacy Chopin preferred in her essays. She first discloses her writing habits—composing on "a lapboard with a block of paper, a stub pen and a bottle of ink . . . [i]n a Morris chair beside the window" (CW, 721). Amplifying an earlier letter, these remarks confirm that, like many other "scribbling women" who lacked a private study, Chopin worked "in the family living room often in the midst of much clatter."[11] But apart from such cosy details, the essay also articulates a serious aesthetic, particularly on the spontaneity of her fiction, although the insistence on her artlessness—which even equates writing with housework—does seem calculated to deflect the criticism she was receiving about *The Awakening.* Remarking on the absence of her "latest book" in the libraries, for example, she comments wittily on her desire not to "offend a possible buyer." Equally coy are her concluding reflections on the intrusions of inquiring newspaper editors. Questions about her children, for example, elicit both a conventional response—"A woman's reluctance to speak of her children has not yet been chronicled"—and a canny dismissal on their behalf: "they'd be simply wild if I dragged them into this." Chopin's reply to a final question is just as delightfully evasive:

> Suppose I do smoke cigarettes? Am I going to tell it out in meeting? Suppose I don't smoke cigarettes. Am I going to admit such a reflection upon my artistic integrity, and thereby bring upon myself the contempt of the guild?
>
> In answering questions in which an editor believes his readers to be interested, the victim cannot take herself too seriously (CW, 723).

The key to this essay, and perhaps to Chopin's defensive stance, is that last sentence. Chopin's concern for her "artistic integrity," even the rebellious pose of the woman writer, was quite genuine. But the attacks she had suffered for the sake of that integrity demanded a self-protective nonchalance. Chopin had understood quite well the message in the rejection of *The Awakening;* she would not "take herself too seriously" in public again.

A contemporary sketch, entitled "A Reflection" (November 1899), is a less personal and more solemn meditation on the same theme—the role of the artist in an alien environment. This little allegory describes the "moving procession" of life, contrasting those whose "vital and responsive energy" keep it going, and those who "grow weary" or "miss step" and "fall out of rank" to contemplate the continuing march. This latter is the fate of the artist, who falls back to see the whole, at the cost of being denied participation in the "ever-pressing multitude." The artist may not share in the excitement of the race, but she alone will know its meaning and recognize its victors.

Though Chopin expressed her dismay so eloquently, she did not cease to write, despite the once popular impression to the contrary.[12] That very November she composed a new short story of considerable power. Indeed, for the next six months, she continued to write at her usual pace of a story every month or so. What is different about this period is that only the last of these six stories could find a publisher. "Ti Démon" (November 1899), for example, was successively refused during that discouraging spring by *Century*, *Atlantic Monthly*, and then *Scribner's*. *Atlantic Monthly* wrote that they were "very sorry"; despite the tale's "excellent craftsmanship . . . the sad note seems to us too much accented to let us keep the story."[13]

Atlantic was not mistaken about the story's mood. Focusing on the consequences of sudden passion and of betrayal, the tale also involves the paradoxical nature of naming, of reputation, and of illusion. Ti Démon's natural goodness has gradually redefined the meaning of his nickname ("little devil") into a synonym for gentleness; but a single, unthinking attack, together with the gossip and outright slander that follow, completely destroys that identity. Ti Démon's name thus overwhelms his very being; as his deadly reputation expands to match it, like Monsieur Michel of "After the Winter," he is believed to be as "bad as they make 'em." Ironically, dreams have provoked Ti Démon to violence. Tardily and tipsily en route to his assignation with his fiancée Marianne, he thinks of her "coming down between the tall rows of white bursting cotton to meet him. The thought was like a vivid picture flashed and imprinted upon his brain." But even as he treasures that sweet vision, he sees Marianne with Aristides. The contrasting images obliterate all but his anger, and "in speechless wrath" he unleashes his "big broad fists that could do the service of sledge hammers." The contradiction of Ti Démon's gentle vision of love precipitates the violent deed that in turn confirms his name and transforms his identity. The power of a name or a dream – or perhaps, more personally, of a scandal – Chopin reminds us, is not to be underestimated.

After a visit that winter to Louisiana, Chopin wrote a rather rambling reflection on "A December Day in Dixie" (January 1900). The next month she sent to *Youth's Companion* a shortened version, "One Day in Winter." The casual note struck in her letter implies her diminishing expectations: "I can't imagine that you will care for this little sketch, or impression of one snowy day last winter when I arrived in Natchitoches, but I send it anyway, hoping that you might."[14] The revised tale focuses on the incongruities that the snow brings to cotton country:

> Snow upon and beneath the moss-draped branches of the forests; snow along the bayou's edges, powdering the low, pointed, thick palmetto growths; white snow and the fields and fields of white cotton bursting from dry bolls.

While the male narrator's traveling companion is full of business, seeing only wasted cotton and the "lazy rascals" who won't pick it, he is overwhelmed by the beauty. In Natchitoches itself, the snow has done more than transform a depressed commodity into "Fairyland"; it has made the people "all stark mad," frolicking like children. The transformation is complete if temporary. The snow, like the imagination, makes us see the world in new ways, and as the concluding personifications of nature suggest, the familiar is refurbished and brightened by such magical interludes.

Chopin's next two stories are disappointing in their reliance on conventional motifs, despite their overall craftsmanship. "Alexandre's Wonderful Experience" (January 23, 1900) shares the magical spirit of the snow sketch as wish-fulfillment: poor, dreamy young Alexan-

dre's act of charity in a hard-nosed business world is, after some trials, richly rewarded. Though the passing satire at the ruthless businessman, Catalan, the vivid evocations of New Orleans, and Alexandre's feverish reveries recall "Nég Créol," the Cinderella resolution is more characteristic of Chopin's early work. Finally, though one should not make too much of the remark, it is hard not to see some self-reference in the narrator's comment on Alexandre: "His ambitious spirit rebelled at the descent. But however ambitious spirits may rebel, they are oftentimes broken." Perhaps the story's magical resolution vents some of Chopin's own dreams about what she must have felt to be a failing career.

The second offers little more depth. "The Gentleman from New Orleans" (February 6, 1900), as the title indicates, returns to a motif Chopin had worked years before. However, there are new twists; the plot turns on a mistaken identity and the gentleman's visit produces not a romance but a reconciliation. Chopin's keen insight on the plight of women is also reflected in the vivid portrait of Millie Parkins Bénoîte: "too faded for her years and showing a certain lack of self assertion which her husband regarded as the perfection of womanliness." But the most interesting aspect of the story is its insistence on the enduring relationship between father and daughter, a motif Chopin explores more searchingly in her next story.

"Charlie" (April 1900) is one of Chopin's longest tales and contains some of her last public meditations on the relationship of men and women and the constraints of conventions. The heroine is seventeen-year-old Charlotte Laborde—Charlie. At her very first appearance, "galloping along the green levee summit on a big black horse, as if pursued by demons," she manifests the spirited nature that characterizes Chopin's most engaging heroines. But Charlie, like all her predecessors, must learn the limits of her freedom.

One of seven motherless daughters, Charlie has been indulged in the liberties of a tomboy, playing the role of that ideal son her father never had. Against her are set her more docile sisters, each an alternate and more typical caricature of both female behavior and the stages of girlhood: the beautiful and gracious belle, Julia; the vain and possessive Amanda; the emotional, sometimes frankly hysterical Irene; Fidelia, who seeks approval by faithful submission; and Paula and Pauline, mischievous and angelic, the sugar and spice of female childhood.

In the tradition of literary tomboys from Alcott's Jo March to McCullers's Frankie, Charlie sets herself apart from such feminine roles. Her blunt confidence and rowdy exploits are, like theirs, as attractive as they are distinctly unfeminine. But when she one day takes her assumed male prerogatives too far—accidentally shooting a young male visitor—her "unnatural" freedom is abruptly curbed. Deprived of her pistol, that symbolic instrument of male agression and authority, she is sent to the convent school in the city to learn better her female destiny.

In the wounding of young Walton, Charlie metaphorically wounds herself in her sudden experience of love. Plunging into a femaleness as stereotyped and wholehearted as her masculinity, Charlie tries "to transform herself from a hoyden to a fascinating young lady." But her extremism produces a caricature, not a mate. At the same time, this overdrawn femininity injures her father, who mildly rebukes her new feminine identity: "Charlie dear, but you know you mustn't think too much about the hands and all that. Take care of the head, too, and the temper." When her father, shortly after, loses his arm in an accident, Charlie abruptly forsakes the pursuit of femininity to become, quite literally, his right arm. And when Walton later rejects her in favor of Julia, Charlie is finally and ironically freed from the dependence that her excessive femininity would inevitably entail.

Like a Shakespearean comic heroine, Charlie enlarges her self by trying on the roles of each sex. Her boyish disguise instills self-confidence even as it vents her recklessness; her feminine garb enlarges her "deeper emotion" while it exorcises her vanity. In discarding her hand creams and giving away her mother's diamond, the prized "magic" ring of her boyish escapades, Charlie signals the end of adolescence. Her disguises are abandoned; she assumes her true self.

But if Charlie's maturation is toward androgyny, it is not unambivalent. Becoming, in time, Les Palmiers' mistress, "with all the dignity and grace which the term implied," Charlie, like Thérèse, one of Chopin's first heroines, exhibits a consciously feminine authority. She is also rewarded with a mate, Mr. Gus. But even as she is assuring Gus of her affection, her father has only to cough for her to hasten to his side. Left by her assurances "in an ecstasy in the moonlight," Gus will allow her to fulfill—in her own good time—her female destiny in marriage. But, as Charlie clearly understands, it is her bond with her father that preserves the freedom and authority she enjoys as his favored surrogate.

"Charlie" essentially represents a compromise of love and independence not unlike that of Chopin's first tale, "Wiser Than a God." So strong was her realism (and finally pessimism) about human institutions that she could not, even after ten years of writing, imagine a fictional equivalent for the independent female within the structures of marriage. Nonetheless, Chopin's portrait of Charlie does extend the efforts of stories like "Athénaïse" to reconcile female personhood and marriage. In that tale, Chopin had relied on the procreative powers of the woman to confirm and establish her individuality. But *The Awakening*, with its volatile implications about sexuality, had demonstrated that route's tragic limitations. "Charlie," written barely a year after the public rebuke of the novel, attempts another approach of masculine imitation, but its caution tends to inhibit insight. That the issue continued to absorb Chopin, that her talent was sufficient — these remain clear; that her courage was failing appears only too likely.

Soon after Chopin finished "Charlie," she wrote "The White Eagle" (May 9, 1900), a brief tale that recalls the evocative prose poetry of "An Egyptian Cigarette." Patently symbolic, it recounts the fortunes of a white cast-iron bird, and the girl whose affection keeps it nearby throughout her declining life. Twice contrasted with seasonal changes, the eagle assumes an aspect of permanence, despite its less and less propitious roles. Passing from a conspicuous place as an emblem of an old homestead, to a child's toy, to a tombstone, the bird remains impassive and mysterious. Attributing life to it as her own declines, the woman often sees the bird blink as she sews, and then in her last fever, it "had blinked and blinked, had left his corner and come and perched upon her, pecking at her bosom."

This final vision and the woman's isolation credit certain sexual dimensions of the eagle's presence, but its meaning can also be related to the familial contexts of its origins. The eagle is a beloved fragment of a beloved past, of possibility and family pride, of those "unconscious summer dreams of a small child." Always proud, the eagle helped the woman "to remember; or better, he never permitted her to forget" the aspirations of that lost time. A cherished burden she cannot discard, the bird ultimately mediates her destruction even as it preserves her memory. Such ambivalence is its defining quality. Perched on a grave, always threatening to "take his flight," he never does. For all his apparent splendor and promise, the white eagle only "gazes across the vast plain with an expression which in a human being would pass for wisdom." The poignant irony of the final image, which culminates a whole pattern of bird imagery in Chopin's work, suffuses this story. The free-flying bird that Edna—and perhaps Chopin as well—tried to imitate, reveals here the nature of its impotence: no longer an emblem of pride or even a shelter of dreams, it is only an earthbound, permanent illusion of flight, pessimistically reaffirming the folly of human aspirations.

Though "An Egyptian Cigarette" had appeared in April and "The White Eagle" soon after in *Vogue*, their acceptance seems to have done little to overcome Chopin's evident timidity before her reading public. After a spring of steady creativity, she wrote only one or two poems that summer of 1900. She had a sudden burst of productivity in mid-October, writing three stories in as many days, but since, of those listed in her notebook, only one survives, we may surmise that they were not very satisfactory.

A likely representative is the remaining story, "The Wood-Choppers" (October 17, 1901), which *Youth's Companion* accepted for its May 1902 issue. A very conventional tale, it is only partially enlivened by its Louisiana setting, which has largely faded to French allusions and some vestiges of dialect. Like Charlie, Léontine presumes under duress to assume a male task, woodchopping. But though she is proud and spunky, she yields rather easily to an insistent male and readily abandons her teaching job for the greater security of marriage.

A later story, "Polly" (January 14, 1902), reiterates this exchange of work for wifehood. Polly, however, is at least a new type in Chopin's canon, a country girl with a city job as a bookkeeper. Like many magazine stories of the 1950s, the principal action is her promotion from that job to wedlock; its substance is a corollary exhibition of Polly's generosity to her family, thanks to an improbable gift from a distant uncle. The story is polished and full of humorous touches, but its insights into human nature tend to be peripheral. The weak joke of its conclusion ("Polly, put the kettle on") suggests the disappointing level of its achievement.

This turned out to be Chopin's final comment in print, appearing in the July 1902 *Youth's Companion.* Its leaden sprightliness aptly characterizes the mood of these last stories, as Chopin attempted to regain her audience by a return to styles and themes she evidently thought more acceptable. The last manuscript story we have is a fragment, begun sometime in 1903, "The Impossible Miss Meadows." Set in the Wisconsin lakes and featuring a very upper-crust family who must accommodate an Irish immigrant for charity's sake, its setting and social strata are new elements in Chopin's fiction. But this bit of sophisticated satire is too incomplete and too isolated to permit any conclusions to be drawn. Chopin appears to have written nothing after it, and throughout 1903 and 1904, her health steadily declined.

Chopin's brief career thus drew to its denouement. From the outset, she had struggled with the dualities that marked her career's close: how does one express one's personal vision in rigid and resisting forms? Chopin's final stories suggest that "what she saw," the primary impulse of her best fiction, had finally yielded to the stage trappings of convention and marketability. Her finest work rejected and a supportive literary community unavailable, she had lost faith in the power of creative insight. But as long as that faith had held, Kate Chopin had produced memorable work, writing nearly two hundred pieces, including two excellent collections of local-color fiction, several dozen superb short stories, and one classic novel.

Focusing in her very earliest fiction on the essential conflict between one's ideals and the hard facts of human life, she had continually explored the uneasy resolutions that result. For Chopin, the keenest expression of the inner self was sexuality, and it came to represent in her fiction the most powerful and disruptive of personal realities. From "A Point at Issue!" and "A Shameful Affair" to "The Storm," Chopin explored the ways in which the repression of this force only intensified the rupture of its external disguises. In "Athénaïse" or "A Vocation and a Voice," or even "Regret" or "A Morning Walk," the recognition of one's sensual being becomes the key to identity and integrity. And that liberation of the self occurs precisely in recognizing the hollowness of conventional surfaces. But while "The Story of an Hour" or "A Pair of Silk Stockings" offers incisive portraits of the desire for integrity, Chopin constantly measures value in costs. As forcefully as she demonstrated the price of repression in "Fedora" or "Her Letters," so she insisted on the difficulties of freedom in tales like "Charlie" or "Lilacs," and especially *The Awakening.* For Chopin, life remained essentially dual, and the ambiguities of tales like "A Respectable Woman," "Nég Créol," "Two Portraits," "An Egyptian Cigarette," or "Madame Celestin's Divorce" only highlight the central feature of her work. Chopin could well see the attractions of freedom and integrity, the value of healthy sensuality and female independence, but she was never unaware of the consequences and limitations of those aspirations: biology, relationships, moral custom, and social order. And in her fiction she tried, by balance and opposition, by ambivalence and candor, to reflect those complexities as precisely as her own limitations as a serious (and thus commercial) artist would permit.

How much her disappointment in the aftermath of *The Awakening* contributed to both her physical and creative decline is matter only for speculation. However, recognizing what she had accomplished in a career of just over a dozen years, and perceiving what she was capable of, we can only agree with Larzer Ziff that the loss to American literature in those, her last disquieting years, was great, a loss as fully lamentable as the early deaths of Stephen Crane and Frank Norris.[15]

Notes

Introduction

1. Per Seyersted summarizes the critical history of Chopin's work in *Kate Chopin: A Critical Biography* (Baton Rouge: Louisiana State University Press, 1969), pp. 186–90. See also Marlene Springer, *Edith Wharton and Kate Chopin: A Reference Guide* (Boston: G. K. Hall and Co., 1976), esp. pp. 188–94.
2. Fred Lewis Pattee, *The Development of the Short Story: A Historical Survey* (New York: Harper and Bros., 1923), pp. 324–27.
3. Daniel S. Rankin, *Kate Chopin and Her Creole Stories* (Philadelpia: University of Pennsylvania, 1932), p. 175ff.
4. Cyrille Arnavon, "Les Débuts du roman réaliste américain et l'influence française," *Romanciers Américains Contemporains*, ed. Henri Kerst, Cahiers des Langues Modernes, I (Paris: Didier, 1946), pp. 9–42. Arnavon's reservations are elaborated in the "Introduction" to his 1952 translation of *The Awakening*, reprinted in *A Kate Chopin Miscellany*, edited by Per Seyersted and Emily Toth (Natchitoches, La.: Northwestern State University Press, 1979), pp. 168–88.
5. Kate Chopin, *The Awakening*, with an introduction by Kenneth Eble (New York: Capricorn Books, 1964).
6. *The Complete Works of Kate Chopin*, edited with an introduction by Per Seyersted (Baton Rouge: Louisiana State University Press, 1969).

1. St. Louis Woman, Louisiana Writer

1. Most of the information in this chapter is drawn from Chopin's biographers, Rankin and Seyersted, as above. Additional information was provided by Emily Toth, whose forthcoming biography will be published by Atheneum.
2. Seyersted, *Biography*, p. 13; see also Elizabeth Shown Mills, "Colorful Characters from Kate's Past," *Kate Chopin Newsletter* 2 (Spring 1976):7–12.
3. See "Brother Tom's Final Ride," *Regionalism and the Female Imagination* 3 (Spring 1977):40; and Mary Helen Wilson, "Kate Chopin's Family: Fallacies and Facts, Including Kate's True Birthdate," *Kate Chopin Newsletter* 2 (Winter 1976–77):25–31. Wilson's later research has also confirmed the birth of Marie Thérèse; however, the 1850 census entry, "Cath. 7/12," that she proposes as evidence of Chopin's birthday probably refers to another Katherine, seven months old at the time of the census, who died before Kate's birth in 1851.
4. Rankin, p. 36.
5. Letter of Sister Garesché, 7 September 1930, as quoted by Rankin, p. 43.
6. *Miscellany*, pp. 54; 55; 59. The original commonplace book is in the Missouri Historical Society, St. Louis.
7. William Schuyler, "Kate Chopin," *The Writer* 8 (August 1894):115–17; reprinted in *Miscellany*, pp. 115–19.
8. *Miscellany*, pp. 62–64.
9. *Miscellany*, p. 67.
10. "Three Months Abroad" in *Miscellany*, pp. 67–87.
11. *Miscellany*, p. 81.
12. *Miscellany*, p. 93.
13. Rankin, pp. 88–89; cf. Seyersted, *Biography*, p. 45 and note.
14. This is the evaluation of Rankin, who saw these "jottings" before their disappearance, p. 92.
15. Rankin, p. 103.
16. Later, in *At Fault*, Chopin alludes to the ghost of "old McFarland," "the person that Mrs. W'at's her name wrote about in Uncle Tom's Cabin" (CW, 751). Today the "Little Eva Plantation" in Chopin, Louisiana, boasts a replica of

the famous cabin. The Bayou Folk Museum, her Louisiana Avenue home in New Orleans, and the McPherson Avenue house in St. Louis remain Chopin's only surviving residences.

17. Rankin, p. 102.
18. Toth has recently confirmed this much disputed date through a clipping at the Missouri Historical Society, but see her earlier "The Practical Side of Oscar Chopin's Death," *Kate Chopin Newsletter* 1 (Winter 1975–76):29.
19. Schuyler, *Miscellany*, p. 117.
20. Toth's biography reviews the evidence for this relationship.
21. Letter of Lelia Chopin Hattersley to L. R. Whipple, 12 November 1907, as quoted by Rankin, p. 35.
22. Rankin, p. 107; Chopin's logbooks, Missouri Historical Society.
23. Rankin, p. 89.
24. Schuyler, *Miscellany*, p. 117.
25. Seyersted, *Biography*, p. 116.
26. [Vernon Knapp?], "Is There an Interesting Woman in St. Louis?" St. Louis *Republic* (11 September 1910), sec. 5, p. 1; in *Miscellany*, p. 151.
27. Letter to Waitman Barbe, 2 October 1894, *Miscellany*, p. 121; and letter to Horace Scudder, 20 January 1897, *Miscellany*, p. 127.
28. As cited by Seyersted in *Biography*, p. 63.
29. Seyersted, *Biography*, p. 175 and note.
30. Letter from W. B. Parker, 18 January 1900, *Miscellany*, p. 148.
31. Letter quoted by Rankin, p. 185; Seyersted, *Biography*, p. 185.

2. *At Fault:* Fictional Debut

1. Chopin's notebooks, Missouri Historical Society; also quoted in Seyersted, *Biography*, p. 52.
2. See Helen White Papashvily's pioneering study, *All the Happy Endings* (New York: Harper and Bros., 1956). The women's movement, led by Elizabeth Cady Stanton, had for twenty years campaigned vigorously for the liberalization of divorce laws. According to the newly kept Bureau

of Census statistics, the rate of divorce, though still small (61 per 1,000 marriages in 1890), had doubled since 1870; see Donald Nelson Koster, *The Theme of Divorce in American Drama, 1871–1939* (Philadelphia: University of Pennsylvania, 1942), p. 5. For a more general study, see Elaine Tyler May, *Great Expectations: Marriage and Divorce in Post-Victorian America* (Chicago: University of Chicago Press, 1980), passim.

3. James Harwood Barnett, *Divorce and the American Divorce Novel, 1858–1937* (1939; reprint ed., New York: Russell and Russell, 1967), p. 35. *The Catholic World* offered essays on divorce in its October 1888 and March 1889 issues, vol. 48, nos. 283 and 288; the reform-minded *Arena* aired the matter in three spring issues of 1890, featuring E. C. Stanton herself in the April number; and the *North American Review* entertained three successive debates from November 1889 to January 1890, the latter including essays by five prominent women writers: Mary A. Livermore, Amelia E. Barr, Rose Terry Cooke, Elizabeth Stuart Phelps, and Jennie June, aka Jane Cunningham Croly; see *The North American Review* 149:5:513–38; 149:6:641–52; and 150:1:110–35.
4. Papishvily observes that among domestic novelists, only T. S. Arthur treated divorce at all until well after the Civil War, *All the Happy Endings*, pp. 150–51. See Mary Jane Holmes's *Daisy Thornton* (1878); Margaret Lee's popular *Divorce* (1882); three novels in 1886—Constance Fenimore Woolson's *East Angels*, Mary G. McClelland's *Princess*, and Anne R. Macfarlanes's *Children of the Earth*—and Madeleine Vinton Dahlgren's *Divorced* (1887). Finally, *The Church Review* reviewed critically the three 1886 novels on divorce, to conclude that only Howells's *A Modern Instance* (1882) had succeeded in being "strictly artistic and rigidly moral"; 48 (November 1886):392–99. See also Barnett's analysis of this topic: Barnett, *Divorce*, pp. 96–104.
5. Larzer Ziff, *The American 1890s: Life and Times of a Lost Generation* (New York: Viking Press, 1966), pp. 279–80.
6. Seyersted, *Biography*, p. 93.
7. See esp. Lewis Leary, "Kate Chopin's Other Novel," in his *Southern Excursions: Essays on Mark Twain and Others*

(Baton Rouge: Louisiana State University Press, 1971), pp. 176–91; Thomas Bonner, Jr., "Kate Chopin's *At Fault* and *The Awakening:* A Study in Structure," *Markham Review* 7 (Fall 1977):10–15; Bernard J. Koloski, "The Structure of Kate Chopin's *At Fault,*" *Studies in American Fiction* 3 (Spring 1975), 89–94; and Seyersted, *Biography,* pp. 118–20. See also Donald A. Ringe, "Cane River World: Kate Chopin's *At Fault* and Related Stories," *Studies in American Fiction* 3 (Autumn 1975):157–66; and Robert D. Arner, "Landscape Symbolism in Kate Chopin's *At Fault,*" *Louisiana Studies* 9 (Fall 1970):142–53.

8. Cable's uncomplimentary fictionalizations of Creoles had caused public outrage in New Orleans in the 1880s; see Louis D. Rubin, Jr., *George Washington Cable: The Life and Times of a Southern Heretic* (New York: Pegasus Press, 1969), p. 98ff.
9. Emily Toth, "St. Louis and the Fiction of Kate Chopin," *Bulletin of the Missouri Historical Society* 32 (October 1975), 33–50.
10. Ronald P. Byars, "The Making of the Self-Made Man: The Development of Masculine Roles and Images in Ante-Bellum America" (Dissertation, Michigan State University, 1979), p. 48.
11. Tony Tanner, *Adultery in the Novel: Contract and Transgression* (Baltimore, Md.: The Johns Hopkins University Press, 1979), p. 15. The domestic themes of James and Howells and later of Wharton, Crane, and Dreiser readily attest to the urgency of the crisis in America; see Joseph Candela, "The Domestic Orientation of American Novels," *American Literary Realism* 13 (Spring 1980):1–18.
12. James found sinister this "growing divorce between the American woman (with her comparative leisure, culture, grace, social instincts, artistic ambitions) and the male American immersed in the ferocity of business, with no time for any but the most sordid business interests, purely commercial, professional, democratic and political"; *The Notebooks*, ed. by F. O. Matthiessen and Kenneth B. Murdock (New York: Oxford, 1947), p. 129.
13. "*At Fault*. A Correction," *The Enterprise* (Natchitoches), 18 December 1890. The anonymous "Review of Mrs. Kate

Chopin's Novel 'At Fault'" had appeared in the issue of 4 December 1890. My thanks to E. Toth for noting this exchange.

14. "Introduction to *Pierre et Jean*" (1887), edited and translated by Lewis Gallantière, *The Portable Maupassant* (New York: Viking Press, 1947), p. 672.
15. The St. Louis *Post-Dispatch*, for example, applauded her for embodying her opinions "in the dialogue, not in the narrative," 5 October 1890, p. 31.
16. See Winfried Flück, "Tentative Transgressions: Kate Chopin's Fiction as a Mode of Symbolic Action," *Studies in American Fiction* 10 (1982):151–71.
17. Kate Chopin's notebooks, Missouri Historical Society. The notebooks indicate other stories now lost, including "Octave Feuillet" (1,200 words; February [?] 1891), sent to Belfords but returned "by req." and submitted to the *Post-Dispatch*, 13 October 1891; "Bambo Pellier" (13,600 words; 25 May 1892), entered in a contest in *Youth's Companion* and returned that November; and a late story, "Millie's First Party" (February 1901), which Chopin indicates sold for $30 – but not to whom.
18. See Susan Wolstenholme, "Kate Chopin's Sources for 'Mrs. Mobry's Reason,'" *American Literature* 51 (January 1980): 540–43.

3. *Bayou Folk:* A Louisiana Local Colorist

1. *Miscellany*, p. 119; p. 195, note 12A; and p. 118.
2. Rankin, p. 132.
3. Interview cited by Seyersted, *Biography*, p. 83 and note; cf. *Miscellany*, p. 90.
4. *Miscellany*, pp. 90–91. Chopin praised Freeman's *Pembroke* (1894) as "the most profound, the most powerful piece of fiction of its kind that has ever come from the American press," and she deplored the critics who had "no feeling for the spirit of the work, the subtle genius which created it"; *Miscellany*, p. 96.
5. The "flattering letter" accompanied a request for revisions; the story was accepted 3 August 1891; Chopin's logbook, Missouri Historical Society. Cf. *Miscellany*, p. 106.
6. *Publisher's Weekly*, 45, no. 11 (17 March 1894):450.

7. Though a letter from Houghton Mifflin in September 1893 requests Chopin's "wishes as to exact order" for her collection, correspondence in December also indicates the publisher's input in the decision to place the "three 'Santien boys' together"; *Miscellany*, pp. 108 and 110.
8. Letter to Gilder, 12 July 1891, *Miscellany*, p. 106.
9. *Miscellany*, p. 90.
10. Chopin's logbook, Missouri Historical Society.
11. See Catherine J. Starke, *Black Portraiture in American Fiction: Stock Characters, Archetypes and Individuals* (New York: Basic Books, 1971), esp. p. 30ff; and Sterling Brown, *The Negro in American Fiction* (Port Washington, N.Y.: Kennikat Press, 1968).
12. Chopin sent it to *Harper's Young People, Wide Awake*, and the New Orleans *Picayune* before giving up; Chopin's logbook, Missouri Historical Society.
13. Pattee, *Development*, p. 327.
14. See Judith R. Berzon, *Neither White nor Black: The Mulatto Character in American Fiction* (New York: New York University Press, 1978), pp. 102–3.
15. *Miscellany*, p. 96.
16. Rankin, p. 134.
17. Rankin, p. 132. The contest was announced in the Sunday *New York Herald*, 20 September 1891, p. 10.
18. *Miscellany*, pp. 95–96.

4. *A Night in Acadie:* The Confidence of Success

1. *Miscellany*, pp. 89 and 96. Seyersted notes a second printing of 500 copies of *Bayou Folk* in May 1895, and two of 150 in 1904 and 1911; the initial printing was of 1,250 copies; *Biography*, p. 210n.
2. "Recent Novels," *The Nation* 58, no. 1513 (28 June 1894): 488; "Recent Fiction," *Atlantic Monthly* 74 (April 1894): 558–59.
3. *Miscellany*, p. 96.
4. "The Western Association of Writers" (June 30, 1894), CW, 691–92. Chopin's remarks followed her attendance at the Association's northern Indiana convention a week earlier; *Miscellany*, p. 97.
5. *Miscellany*, p. 92.

6. Chopin's logbooks, Missouri Historical Society.
7. Seyersted, *Biography*, p. 58.
8. See *Century* 48 (July 1894):469–70 and 48 (August 1894): 605–23; see also Arthur John, *The Best Years of the Century: R. W. Gilder, Scribner's Monthly, and the Century Magazine, 1870–1909* (Urbana: University of Illinois Press, 1981), pp. 218–19.
9. Letter to J. M. Stoddart, 31 March 1895, *Miscellany*, pp. 123–24.
10. *Miscellany*, pp. 92–93.
11. Both "The Night Came Slowly" and "Juanita" (originally "Annie Venn") were first written in Chopin's diary while she was vacationing at "The Cedars," a popular Missouri retreat; cf. *Miscellany*, pp. 97–99; and Seyersted, *Biography*, p. 217, note 4.
12. Cf. letters in *Miscellany*, pp. 123–24; Chopin's list names "A Divorce Case," "Mad," "It," "Solitude," "Night," and "Suicides." Logbooks, Missouri Historical Society.
13. These articles are dated 1892 in Chopin's logbook but were published in the spring of 1891: "The Shape of the Head," St. Louis *Post-Dispatch*, 25 January 1891; "Revival of Wrestling," St. Louis *Post-Dispatch*, 8 March 1891; and "How to Make Mannikins," St. Louis *Post-Dispatch*, 5 April 1891 ("Cut Paper Figures" in her log). Chopin's log on the same page notes three other apparent translations, unlocated and presumably from the same period: "A Visit to the Planet Mars" (March 8); "A Trip to Portuguese Guinea" (February 27); and "Transfusion of Goatsblood" (March 23).
14. Letter to Waitman Barbe, *Miscellany*, p. 120.
15. "More Novels," *Nation* 66 (9 June 1898):477; "Mrs. Chopin's *Night in Acadie*," *Critic* 29 (16 April 1898):266; and *The Mirror* (25 November 1897):5–6. This article is reprinted by John L. Idol, Jr., in "A Note on William Marion Reedy and Kate Chopin," *Missouri Historical Society Bulletin* 30 (October 1973):57–58.
16. *Miscellany*, p. 110.
17. These tales include "Madame Célestin's Divorce," "A Lady of Bayou St. John," "La Belle Zoraïde," and "At Chênière Caminada."
18. Gouvernail reappears in both "Athénaïse" and *The Awak-*

ening. See Joyce Dyer, "Gouvernail: Kate Chopin's Sensitive Bachelor," *Southern Literary Journal* 14 (Fall 1981): 46–55.

19. See Lewis Leary, "Kate Chopin and Walt Whitman," *Walt Whitman Review* 16 (December 1970):120–21.
20. Letter from R. E. Lee Gibson, 26 February 1899, *Miscellany*, pp. 130–31.
21. Compare "At the 'Cadian Ball," "A Visit to Avoyelles," "Ma'ame Pélagie," and "Desirée's Baby," which immediately precede the composition of "Caline." See Josephine Donovan, *Sarah Orne Jewett* (New York: Ungar, 1980), p. 138.
22. *Miscellany*, p. 94.
23. Col. Robert G. Ingersoll, "An Agnostic's View," *North American Review* 149 (November 1889):131;136.
24. See Robert D. Arner, "Kate Chopin," *Louisiana Studies* 14 (Spring 1975): 11–139; Joyce Ruddell Ladenson, "The Return of St. Louis' Prodigal Daughter: Kate Chopin after Seventy Years," *Midamerica* 2 (1975):24–34; Ziff, *The American 1890s*, p. 299; and Toth, "The Independent Woman," p. 655.
25. Seyersted, *Biography*, p. 73. In a January 1896 letter to Stone and Kimball Chopin writes: "These things ['Lilacs,' 'Three (sic) Portraits,' and two poems] have not been printed. I would greatly like to see one of them – some of them – something – anything – over my name in the *Chap-Book*"; *Miscellany*, p. 125. Chopin's log indicates that she submitted at least eight of her stories to the journal without a single acceptance.
26. Helen Taylor, "Introduction," *Kate Chopin: Portraits* (London: The Women's Press, 1979), pp. vii–xix. Cf. Toth, "Independent Woman," p. 655.
27. Seyersted concludes that "Vagabonds" "describes an actual incident in the life of Kate Chopin, the Cloutierville widow"; *Biography*, p. 217, note 4; see also Arner, "Characterization and the Colloquial Style in Kate Chopin's 'Vagabonds,'" *Markham Review* 2 (May 1971): 110–112.
28. Letter to *Century*, 5 January 1897, *Miscellany*, p. 127.

5. Realizations: *A Vocation and a Voice*

1. See the letters to Houghton Mifflin and J. M. Stoddart of Lippincott's, pp. 123–24; letters to Stone and Kimball, p. 125; and notes pp. 196–97 in *Miscellany*.
2. Chopin's log notes, Missouri Historical Society. Though Rankin felt that her publishers were intimidated by *The Awakening*'s reception, p. 195, Seyersted suggests that Chopin's new collection was the victim of an unrelated reduction in titles, *Biography*, p. 182.
3. Arner, "Kate Chopin," p. 79, and Rankin, p. 195.
4. See the essay, "As You Like It," and her stories "The Wizard of Gettysburg," "Tante Cat'rinette," "Madame Martel's Christmas Eve," and "An Egyptian Cigarette"; see also Seyersted, *Biography*, p. 216, note 39.
5. *Miscellany*, p. 128.
6. *Miscellany*, p. 92.
7. See, for example, "Love on the Bon-Dieu," "After the Winter," or "At Chênière Caminada."
8. The most important instance of this vogue is Stuart Merrill's collected translations, *Pastels in Prose*, with a laudatory introduction by W. D. Howells (New York: Harper and Bros., 1890).
9. See George Sand, *Letters of a Traveller*, trans. Eliza A. Ashurst (London: E. Churton, 1847), I:52; and Charles Baudelaire, "L'Invitation au Voyage," from *Le Spleen de Paris* (1869) in *Oeuvres Complètes de Baudelaire*, ed. Y-G. le Dantec and C. Pichois (Editions Gallimard, 1965), pp. 253–55.

6. *The Awakening*

1. Cynthia Griffin Wolff, "Thanatos and Eros: Kate Chopin's *The Awakening*," *American Quarterly* 25 (October 1973): 449–71; and Donald A. Ringe, "Romantic Imagery in Kate Chopin's *The Awakening*," *American Literature* 43 (January 1972):580–88. See also Ruth Sullivan and Stewart Smith, "Narrative Stance in Kate Chopin's *The Awakening*," *Studies in American Fiction* 1 (Spring 1973):62–75, who stress the complexity of Chopin's point of view.

2. Otis B. Wheeler, "The Five Awakenings of Edna Pontellier," *Southern Review* 11 (January 1975):118–28; Stanley Kauffmann, "The Really Lost Generation," *The New Republic* 155 (3 December 1966):22; 37–38; Patricia Hopkins Latin, "Childbirth and Motherhood in Kate Chopin's Fiction," *Regionalism and the Female Imagination* 4 (Spring 1978):8–12; and Irene Dash, "The Literature of Birth and Abortion," *Regionalism and the Female Imagination* 3 (Spring 1977):8–13; Seyersted, *Biography*, p. 148; Lawrence Thornton, "*The Awakening*: A Political Romance," *American Literature* 52 (March 1980):50–66.
3. Seyersted, *Biography*, p. 149; and Suzanne Wolkenfeld, "Edna's Suicide: The Problem of the One and the Many," *The Awakening*, ed. Margaret Culley (New York: Norton, 1976), pp. 218–224. See also George M. Spangler, "Kate Chopin's *The Awakening*: A Partial Dissent," *Novel* 3 (Spring 1970):249–55.
4. Elaine Showalter, "Feminist Criticism in the Wilderness," in *Writing and Sexual Difference*, ed. Elizabeth Abel (Chicago: University of Chicago Press, 1982), pp. 9–35.
5. See Elaine Jasenas, "The French Influence in Kate Chopin's *The Awakening*," *Nineteenth Century French Studies* 4 (Spring 1976):312–22; or Sandra M. Gilbert, "The Second Coming of Aphrodite: Kate Chopin's Fantasy of Desire," *The Kenyon Review* n.s. 5 (Summer 1983):42–66.
6. See Robert S. Levine, "Circadian Rhythms in Kate Chopin's *The Awakening*," *Studies in American Fiction* 10 (Spring 1982):71–81.
7. John R. May, "Local Color in *The Awakening*," *Southern Review* 6 (Fall 1970):1031–1040.
8. Paula A. Treichler, "The Construction of Ambiguity in *The Awakening:* A Linguistic Analysis," in *Woman and Language in Literature and Society*, ed. Sally McConnell-Ginet (New York: Praeger, 1980), pp. 239–57.
9. Seyersted, *Biography*, p. 179; and *Miscellany*, pp. 145–47.
10. Anne Goodwyn Jones, *Tomorrow Is Another Day: The Woman Writer in the South, 1859–1936* (Baton Rouge: Louisiana State University Press, 1981), p. 168.
11. The classical overtones of the final scene are mentioned by Seyersted, p. 158, and Kenneth Eble, "Introduction," *The*

Awakening (New York: Capricorn Books, 1964), pp. v–xiv; see also Wolff, "Thanatos and Eros," p. 469; and Ringe, "Romantic Imagery," p. 587.

12. Frances Porcher, "Kate Chopin's Novel," *The Mirror* 9 (4 May 1899):6; reprinted in the Culley edition, pp. 145–46.
13. "Notes from Bookland," St. Louis *Globe-Democrat*, 4 May 1899, p. 5; reprinted in Culley, pp. 146–47; and "Kate Chopin's Novel," St. Louis *Post-Dispatch*, 21 May 1899, p. 6.
14. C. L. Deyo, "The Newest Books," St. Louis *Post-Dispatch*, 20 May 1899, p. 4; reprinted in Culley, pp. 147–49.
15. "New Publications," New Orleans *Times-Democrat*, 18 June 1899, p. 15; reprinted in Culley, p. 150.
16. "Sibert" [Willa Cather], "Books and Magazines," Pittsburgh *Leader*, 8 July 1899, p. 6; reprinted in Culley, pp. 153–55; and "Fresh Literature," Los Angeles *Sunday Times*, 25 June 1899, p. 12; reprinted in Culley, p. 152.
17. *Book News* 17 (July 1899):612; in *Miscellany*, p. 137.
18. As cited by Seyersted, *Biography*, p. 178.

7. Poems and Final Stories: Epilogues

1. Chopin had sent *The Awakening* to Way and Williams of Chicago on January 21, 1898; but before it was published, Stone and Kimball, who also produced the *Chap-Book*, bought the firm. *The Awakening* was published by Herbert S. Stone the next year.
2. Seyersted's dating of the poems is noted parenthetically in the text; question marks indicate his best conjecture.
3. Letter to Waitman Barbe, *Miscellany*, p. 120.
4. Seyersted, *Biography*, p. 225, note 42.
5. The poem is referred to as "Then Wouldst Thou Know" in a letter to Stone and Kimball, 2 January 1896, *Miscellany*, p. 125.
6. Seyersted, *Biography*, p. 85.
7. Refused by several magazines, including *Century*, the manuscript suggests she continued revising and evidently renamed it late in 1899 in order to use its original title, "Ti Démon," for a new story; see her letter to *Century*, 1

December 1899; *Miscellany*, pp. 147–48 and her notebooks, Missouri Historical Society.

8. Seyersted, *Biography*, p. 164.
9. See Seyersted, *Biography*, pp. 164–69; and Pamela Gaudé "Kate Chopin's 'The Storm': A Study of Maupassant's Influence," *Kate Chopin Newsletter* 1 (Fall 1975):1–6.
10. St. Louis *Post-Dispatch*, 26 November 1899, sec. 4, p. 1.
11. See the letter to Waitman Barbe, *Miscellany*, p. 120.
12. See Rankin's comments, pp. 185–86.
13. Letter from W. B. Parker, 18 January 1900, *Miscellany*, p. 148.
14. Letter to *Youth's Companion*, 15 February 1900, *Miscellany*, p. 148.
15. Ziff, *The American 1890s*, p. 305.

Bibliography

Works by Kate Chopin

At Fault. St. Louis: Nixon-Jones Printing Co., 1890.

Bayou Folk. Boston: Houghton Mifflin & Co., 1894. Contents: "A No-Account Creole," "In and Out of Old Natchitoches," "In Sabine," "A Very Fine Fiddle," "Beyond the Bayou," "Old Aunt Peggy," "The Return of Alcibiade," "A Rude Awakening," "The Bênitous' Slave," "Désirée's Baby," "A Turkey Hunt," "Madame Célestin's Divorce," "Love on the Bon-Dieu," "Loka," "Boulôt and Boulotte," "For Marse Chouchoute," "A Visit to Avoyelles," "A Wizard from Gettysburg," "Ma'ame Pélagie," "At the 'Cadian Ball," "La Belle Zoraïde," "A Gentleman of Bayou Têche," "A Lady of Bayou St. John."

A Night in Acadie. Chicago: Way & Williams, 1897. Contents: "A Night in Acadie," "Athénaïse," "After the Winter," "Polydore," "Regret," "A Matter of Prejudice," "Caline," "A Dresden Lady in Dixie," "Nég Créol," "The Lilies," "Azélie," "Mamouche," "A Sentimental Soul," "Dead Men's Shoes," "At Chênière Caminada," "Odalie Misses Mass," "Cavanelle," "Tante Cat'rinette," "A Respectable Woman," "Ripe Figs," "Ozème's Holiday."

The Awakening. Chicago and New York: Herbert S. Stone and Co., 1899.

The Complete Works of Kate Chopin. Edited by Per Seyersted. Baton Rouge: Louisiana State University Press, 1969.

Selected Biographical Sources

Mills, Elizabeth. "Colorful Characters from Kate's Past." *Kate Chopin Newsletter* 2 (Spring 1976):7–12.

Rankin, Daniel S. *Kate Chopin and Her Creole Stories*. Philadelphia: University of Pennsylvania Press, 1932.

Seyersted, Per. *Kate Chopin: A Critical Biography*. Baton Rouge: Louisiana State University Press, 1969.

Toth, Emily. *Kate Chopin: A Solitary Soul*. New York: Atheneum, [1986].

______. "Brother Tom's Final Ride." *Regionalism and the Female Imagination* 3 (Spring 1977):40. [Published without attribution.]

______. "Kate Chopin's Music." *Regionalism and the Female Imagination* 3 (Spring 1977):28–29.

______. "The Practical Side of Oscar Chopin's Death." *Kate Chopin Newsletter* 1 (Winter 1975–76):29. [Published without attribution.]

Wilson, Mary Helen. "Kate Chopin's Family: Fallacies and Facts, Including Kate's True Birthdate." *Kate Chopin Newsletter* 2 (Winter 1976–77):25–31.

Selected Bibliographies

Bonner, Thomas, Jr. "Kate Chopin: An Annotated Bibliography." *Bulletin of Bibliography* 32 (July–September 1975):101–5.

Inge, Tonette Bond. "Kate Chopin." In *American Women Writers: Bibliographical Essays*, edited by Maurice Duke *et al.*, pp. 47–69. Westport, Conn.: Greenwood Press, 1983.

Potter, Richard. "Kate Chopin and Her Critics: An Annotated Checklist." *Missouri Historical Society Bulletin* 26 (July 1970):306–17.

Seyersted, Per. "Kate Chopin (1851–1904)." *American Literary Realism* 3 (Spring 1970):153–59.

Springer, Marlene, ed. *Edith Wharton and Kate Chopin: A Reference Guide*. Boston: G. K. Hall & Co., 1976.

______. "Kate Chopin: A Reference Guide Updated." *Resources for American Literary Study* 11 (1981):25–42.

Toth, Emily. "Bibliography of Writings on Kate Chopin." In *A Kate Chopin Miscellany*, edited by Per Seyersted, pp. 212–61. Natchitoches, La.: Northwestern State University Press, 1979.

Selected Criticism

Allen, Priscilla. "Old Critics and New: The Treatment of Chopin's *The Awakening*." In *The Authority of Experience: Essays in Feminist Criticism*, edited by Arlyn Diamond and Lee R. Edwards, pp. 224–38. Amherst: University of Massachusetts Press, 1977.

Arnavon, Cyrille. "Les Débuts du roman réaliste américain et l'influence française." In *Romanciers Américains Contemporains*, edited by Henri Kerst, pp. 9–42. Cahiers des Langues Modernes, I, Paris: Didier, 1946.

Arner, Robert D. "Characterization and the Colloquial Style in Kate Chopin's 'Vagabonds.'" *Markham Review* 2 (May 1971):110–12.

______. "Kate Chopin" [Special Issue]. *Louisiana Studies* 14 (Spring 1975):11–139.

______. "Landscape Symbolism in Kate Chopin's *At Fault*." *Louisiana Studies* 9 (Fall 1970):142–53.

______. "Pride and Prejudice: Kate Chopin's 'Desiree's Baby.'" *Mississippi Quarterly* 25 (1972):131–40.

Bender, Bert. "Kate Chopin's Lyrical Short Stories." *Studies in Short Fiction* 11 (Summer 1974):257–66.

Bonner, Thomas, Jr. "Christianity and Catholicism in the Fiction of Kate Chopin." *Southern Quarterly* 20 (Winter 1982):118–25.

______. "Kate Chopin's *At Fault* and *The Awakening*: A Study in Structure." *Markham Review* 7 (Fall 1977):10–15.

______. "Kate Chopin's European Consciousness." *American Literary Realism, 1870–1910* 8 (1975):281–84.

______. "Kate Chopin: Tradition and the Moment." In *Southern Literature in Transition: Heritage and Promise*, edited by Philip Castille and William Osborne, pp. 141–49. Memphis: Memphis State University Press, 1983.

Candela, Gregory L. "Walt Whitman and Kate Chopin: A Further Connection." *Walt Whitman Review* 24 (1978): 163–65.

Cantwell, Robert. "*The Awakening* by Kate Chopin." *Georgia Review* 10 (Winter 1956):489–94.

Casale, Ottavio Mark. "Beyond Sex: The Dark Romanticism of Kate Chopin's *The Awakening.*" *Ball State University Forum* 19 (Winter 1978):76–80.

Christ, Carol P. *Diving Deep and Surfacing: Women Writers on Spiritual Quest* (Boston: Beacon Press, 1980), esp. pp. 27–40.

Culley, Margaret, ed. "*The Awakening*": *An Authoritative Text, Contexts, Criticism*. New York: W. W. Norton and Co., 1976.

Dash, Irene. "The Literature of Birth and Abortion." *Regionalism and the Female Imagination* 3 (Spring 1977):8–13.

Donovan, Josephine. "Feminist Style Criticism." In *Images of Women in Fiction: Feminist Perspectives*, edited by Susan Koppelman Cornillon, pp. 344–48. Bowling Green: Popular Press, 1972.

Dyer, Joyce Coyne. "Gouvernail, Kate Chopin's Sensitive Bachelor." *Southern Literary Journal* 14 (Fall 1981):46–55.

______. "Kate Chopin's Sleeping Bruties." *Markham Review* 10 (Fall–Winter 1980):10–15.

______. "Night Images in the Work of Kate Chopin." *American Literary Realism, 1870–1910* 14 (Autumn 1981): 216–30.

______. "Restive Brute: The Symbolic Presentation of Repression in Kate Chopin's 'Fedora.'" *Studies in Short Fiction* 15 (Summer 1981):261–65.

Eble, Kenneth. "A Forgotten Novel: Kate Chopin's *The Awakening.*" *Western Humanities Review* 10 (Summer 1956): 261–69. Reprinted in Culley, Margaret, "*The Awakening*": *An Authoritative Text, Contexts, Criticism*.

Fletcher, Marie. "The Southern Woman in the Fiction of Kate Chopin." *Louisiana History* 7 (Spring 1966):117–32. Reprinted in Culley, Margaret, "*The Awakening*": *An Authoritative Text, Contexts, Criticism*.

Flück, Winfried. "Tentative Transgressions: Kate Chopin's Fiction as a Mode of Symbolic Action." *Studies in American Fiction* 10 (Autumn 1982):151–71.

Fox-Genovese, Elizabeth. "Kate Chopin's *The Awakening.*" *Southern Studies* 18 (1979):261–90.

Gardiner, Elaine. "'Ripe Figs': Kate Chopin in Miniature." *Modern Fiction Studies* 28 (Autumn 1982):379–82.

Gaudé, Pamela. "Kate Chopin's 'The Storm': A Study of Maupassant's Influence." *Kate Chopin Newsletter* 1 (Fall 1975):1–6.

Gilbert, Sandra M. "The Second Coming of Aphrodite: Kate Chopin's Fantasy of Desire." *The Kenyon Review* n.s. 5 (Summer 1983):42–66.

Hirsch, Marianne. "Spiritual *Bildung:* The Beautiful Soul as Paradigm." In *The Voyage In: Fictions of Female Development*, edited by Elizabeth Abel, Marianne Hirsch, and Elizabeth Langland, pp. 23–48. Hanover, N.H.: For Dartmouth College by University Press of New England, 1983.

House, Elizabeth Balkman. "*The Awakening:* Kate Chopin's 'Endlessly Rocking' Cycle." *Ball State University Forum* 20 (Spring 1979):53–58.

Howell, Elmo. "Kate Chopin and the Creole Country." *Louisiana History* 20 (1979):209–19.

______. "Kate Chopin and the Pull of Faith: A Note on 'Lilacs.'" *Southern Studies* 18 (1979):103–9.

Huf, Linda A. "*The Awakening* (1899): Kate Chopin's Crimes against Polite Society." In *A Portrait of the Artist as a Young Woman: The Writer as Heroine in American Literature*. New York: Ungar, 1983, pp. 59–79.

Jasenas, Elaine. "The French Influence in Kate Chopin's *The Awakening.*" *Nineteenth-Century French Studies* 4 (Spring 1976):312–22.

Jones, Anne Goodwyn. *Tomorrow Is Another Day: The Woman Writer in the South 1859–1936*. Baton Rouge: Louisiana State University Press, 1981.

Justus, James H. "The Unawakening of Edna Pontellier." *Southern Literary Journal* 10 (Spring 1978):107–22.

Kauffmann, Stanley. "The Really Lost Generation." *New Republic* 155 (3 December 1966):22, 37–38.

Klemans, Patricia A. "The Courageous Soul: Woman as Artist in American Literature." *CEA Critic* 43 (Winter 1981): 39–43.

Koloski, Bernard J. "The Structure of Kate Chopin's *At Fault.*" *Studies in American Fiction* 3 (Spring 1975):89–94.

Ladenson, Joyce Ruddel. "The Return of St. Louis' Prodigal

Daughter: Kate Chopin after Seventy Years." *Midamerica* 2 (1975):24–34.

Lattin, Patricia Hopkins. "Childbirth and Motherhood in Kate Chopin's Fiction." *Regionalism and the Female Imagination* 4 (Spring 1978):8–12.

______. "Kate Chopin's Repeating Characters." *Mississippi Quarterly* 33 (1979–80):19–37.

______. "The Search for Self in Kate Chopin's Fiction: Simple versus Complex Vision." *Southern Studies* 21 (1982): 222–235.

Leary, Lewis. "Kate Chopin and Walt Whitman." *Walt Whitman Review* 16 (December 1970):120–21. Reprinted in Culley, Margaret, *"The Awakening": An Authoritative Text, Contexts, Criticism.*

______. "Kate Chopin's Other Novel." *Southern Literary Journal* 1 (Autumn 1968):6–74. Reprinted in his *Southern Excursions: Essays on Mark Twain and Others*, pp. 176–91. Baton Rouge: Louisiana State University Press, 1971.

______. "Kate Chopin's *The Awakening*." In *Southern Excursions: Essays on Mark Twain and Others*, pp. 159–75. Baton Rouge: Louisiana State University Press, 1971.

Leder, Priscilla. "An American Dilemma: Cultural Conflict in Kate Chopin's *The Awakening*." *Southern Studies* 22 (1983):97–104.

Levine, Robert S. "Circadian Rhythms and Rebellion in Kate Chopin's *The Awakening*." *Studies in American Fiction* 10 (Spring 1982):71–81.

Lohafer, Susan. "'Athénaïse' by Kate Chopin." In *Coming to Terms with the Short Story*, pp. 113–33. Baton Rouge: Louisiana State University Press, 1983.

May, John R. "Local Color in *The Awakening*." *Southern Review* 6 (Autumn 1970):1031–40. Reprinted in Culley, Margaret, *"The Awakening": An Authoritative Text, Contexts, Criticism.*

Mayer, Charles W. "Isabel Archer, Edna Pontellier, and the Romantic Self." *Research Studies* [Washington State University] 47 (1979):89–97.

Miner, M. M. "Veiled Hints: An Affective Stylist's Reading of Kate Chopin's 'Story of an Hour.'" *Markham Review* 11 (Winter 1983):29–32.

Paulsen, Anne-Lise Strømness. "The Masculine Dilemma in Kate Chopin's *The Awakening*." *Southern Studies* 18 (1979):381–424.

Ringe, Donald A. "Cane River World: Kate Chopin's *At Fault* and Related Stories." *Studies in American Fiction* 3 (Autumn 1975):157–66. Reprinted in Culley, Margaret, *"The Awakening": An Authoritative Text, Contexts, Criticism.*

______. "Romantic Imagery in Kate Chopin's *The Awakening*." *American Literature* 43 (January 1972):580–88.

Rocks, James E. "Kate Chopin's Ironic Vision." *Révue de Louisiane/Louisiana Review* (Winter 1972):110–20.

Rogers, Nancy E. "Echoes of George Sand in Kate Chopin." *Revue de Littérature Comparée* 57 (1983):25–42.

Rosowski, Susan J. "The Novel of Awakening." *The Voyage In: Fictions of Female Development*, edited by Elizabeth Abel, Marianne Hirsch, and Elizabeth Langland, pp. 49–68. Hanover, N.H.: For Dartmouth College by University Press of New England, 1983.

Shillingsburg, Miriam J. "The Ascent of Woman, Southern Style: Hentz, King, Chopin." In *Southern Literature in Transition: Heritage and Promise*, edited by Philip Castille and William Osborne, pp. 127–40. Memphis: Memphis State University Press, 1983.

Skaggs, Peggy. "The Boy's Quest in Kate Chopin's 'A Vocation and a Voice.'" *American Literature* 51 (May 1979): 270–76.

______. "'The Man-Instinct of Possession': A Persistent Theme in Kate Chopin's Stories." *Louisiana Studies* 14 (Fall 1975):277–85.

______. "Three Tragic Figures in Kate Chopin's *The Awakening*." *Louisiana Studies* 13 (Winter 1974):345–64.

Spacks, Patricia Meyer. *The Female Imagination*. New York: Knopf, 1975.

Spangler, George. "Kate Chopin's *The Awakening:* A Partial Dissent." *Novel: A Forum on Fiction* 3 (Spring 1970): 249–55. Reprinted in Culley, Margaret, *"The Awakening": An Authoritative Text, Contexts, Criticism.*

Sullivan, Ruth, and Stewart Smith. "Narrative Stance in Kate Chopin's *The Awakening*." *Studies in American Fiction* 1 (1973):62–75.

Thornton, Lawrence. "*The Awakening*: A Political Romance." *American Literature* 52 (March 1980):50–66.

Toth, Emily. "The Cult of Domesticity and 'A Sentimental Soul.'" *Kate Chopin Newsletter* 1 (Fall 1975):9–16.

———. "The Independent Woman and 'Free' Love." *Massachusetts Review* 16 (Autumn 1975):647–64.

———. "Kate Chopin and Literary Convention: 'Désirée's Baby.'" *Southern Studies* 20 (Summer 1981):201–8.

———. "St. Louis and the Fiction of Kate Chopin." *Missouri Historical Society Bulletin* 32 (October 1975):33–50.

Treichler, Paula A. "The Construction of Ambiguity in *The Awakening*: A Linguistic Analysis." In *Woman and Language in Literature and Society*, edited by Sally McConnell-Ginet, pp. 239–57. New York: Praeger, 1980.

Walker, Nancy. "Feminist or Naturalist: The Social Context of Kate Chopin's *The Awakening*." *Southern Quarterly* 17 (1979):95–103.

Wheeler, Otis B. "The Five Awakenings of Edna Pontellier." *Southern Review* 11 (January 1975):118–28.

Wilson, Edmund. *Patriotic Gore: Studies in the Literature of the American Civil War*. New York: Oxford University Press, 1962.

Wolff, Cynthia Griffin. "Kate Chopin and the Fiction of Limits: 'Désirée's Baby.'" *Southern Literary Journal* 10 (Spring 1978):123–33.

———. "Thanatos and Eros: Kate Chopin's *The Awakening*." *American Quarterly* 25 (October 1973):449–71. Reprinted in Culley, Margaret, *"The Awakening": An Authoritative Text, Contexts, Criticism*.

Wolkenfeld, Suzanne. "Edna's Suicide: The Problem of the One and the Many." In *"The Awakening": An Authoritative Text, Contexts, Criticism*, edited by Margaret Culley, pp. 218–24. New York: Norton, 1976.

Wolstenholme, Susan. "Kate Chopin's Sources for 'Mrs. Mobry's Reason.'" *American Literature* 51 (January 1980): 540–43.

Wood, Anne Douglas. "The Literature of Impoverishment: Women Local Colorists in America 1865–1914." *Women's Studies* 1 (1972):3–46.

Wymard, Eleanor B. "Kate Chopin: Her Existential Imagination." *Southern Studies* 19 (Winter 1980):373–84.

Ziff, Larzer. *The American 1890s: Life and Times of a Lost Generation*. New York: The Viking Press, 1966.

Zlotnick, Joan. "A Woman's Will: Kate Chopin on Selfhood, Wifehood, and Motherhood." *Markham Review* 3 (October 1968):1–5.

Index